BRIDGING
THE
CHASM

BRIDGING
THE
CHASM

MARK WILKERSON

ARPress
ILLUMINATING IDEAS.
EMPOWERING VOICES

ARPress
45 Dan Road Suite 5
Canton MA 02021

Hotline: 1(888) 821-0229
Fax: 1(508) 545-7580

Ordering Information:
Quantity sales. Special discounts are available on quantity purchases by corporations, associations, and others. For details, contact the publisher at the address above.

Printed in the United States of America.

ISBN-13:	Softcover	979-8-89356-355-9
	eBook	979-8-89356-356-6

Library of Congress Control Number: 2024905442

CONTENTS

DEDICATION

To my parents for thier love and sacrifice throughout the years, Dad would probably have his fingers over his eyes saying What's Mark doing now. To my brothers and sisters who might be thinking the same thing and to my beautiful wife for her love and patience throughout this journey. For everyone who has ever worked at the Hoover Dam and for all the guides, past and present at Hoover Dam who tell the story of the construction of an American Icon and bring a smile to countless visitors from all over the world amazed at what America could do generations ago when times were bleak during the Great Depression.

CHAPTER 1

Bountiful Dreams—Fall, 1905

S ome of my fondest memories as a child were outside the home breathing the fresh air, walking the hills and valleys, admiring the smell of fresh crops and appreciating Mother Nature at her finest. A most gratifying experience was had as we (my brother Mickey and Susan, whom I secretly adored) sauntered down the valley to our favorite fishing hole.

Before it became a placid pond it was a quite turbulent stream, mostly in late spring or early summer. The snows of the Rockies melted and prompted many destructive floods along the Rio Colorado, the Spanish word for the Colorado River. Entrepreneurs realized the potential of trying to control the river and bring the desirable waters from it to irrigate southern California farmland. Our town, Emmitville, basically grew from a few families to several dozen because of dikes, ditches and canals dug by the Southern California Land Trust Co.

Geographically, Emmitville was located on a huge depression called the Salton Sink, which was part of the Pacific Ocean millions of years ago. Situated at the most northern point of this bowl, this small town and surrounding farms were placated when questions of survival surfaced if a flood were to occur. This advantageous position would according to them let us continue to plant and harvest with confidence. Some were still skeptical including my parents who knew from experience what the Rio Colorado could do.

We had many dreams of ample crops nourished by the man-controlled river. We were told it would provide growth and prosperity for generations for our land in Southern California. We were to learn shortly that the companies furnishing the means to control the river shortchanged the engineering aspects of those control facilities. We were all naïve to think that man could control Mother Nature, never had before and maybe never would.

This particular morning, we (myself, Mickey, Susan and Jim, an Indian friend of Susan) congregated at Bob's farm market, the local general store. A path behind the store would direct us to the fishing pond/swimming hole, whichever whim appealed that day. All of us being young (8-10), swimming mostly was the choice as most days it was hot and dry. It was a good running stream that jig-sawed its way down the valley till the energy was extinguished several miles downstream. The creation of this pond became apparent if one looked in a southwesterly direction. There was a fairly large dam made of wood, twigs, branches, mud and leaves. The falling water of Mother Nature was corralled by another member of Mother Nature. Two beavers dammed up the stream, their engineering was excellent and created a new environment full of fish, birds and small aquatic life. A smile came upon my face when I viewed the vista now. A change for the present that brought several benefits for animal and man alike. New life sprung up as the former stream calmed down. I think my fate was determined during those visits early in life as I viewed the engineering aspects of a couple of animals to control and transform a small part of Mother Nature.

We had gathered in front of the general store and were waiting for Susan's friend Jim. Dave suggested we get a few worms for the fishing pole he brought with him. "I'll need some live bait to catch some fish, so lets go inside Bob's, Mickey you stay outside and wait for Jim." "Why don't you stay outside" quipped Mickey "I'll go inside with Susan and look for your worms." "You would like that wouldn't you but since I'm the oldest Mom said you do as I say" Mickey sure did not like the fact that he was just 1 year younger. He was sure Susan liked him better but the fact that Dave brought up Mom rankled him. "C'mon Susan, Mickey will watch for Jim and then we'll all go down to the swimming hole and do some fishing too" as Dave led Susan into Bob's General store.

As they waited the town was beginning to come to life. Bob's store was slowly filling with farmers picking up or awaiting news for their orders for grain, tools or machinery. Turning what was once desert wasteland into now, with the help of the Colorado River and irrigation into a slowly developing cornucopia. Strawberries, corn, tomatoes, alfafa, wheat, barly, oranges, pecans, almonds, squash, cabbage, etc., with plentiful water almost anything could be grown. "You sure you want to go fishing?' Susan asked as she wandered around the store "I'd just be happy for a good ole swim on this hot day." "That's when the fishing is good plus I just got this new pole, want to try it out at this special place I found" Dave responded as he eyed some good fat worms in a corner wooden small box. "Eeew, don't know how you can put your hands into that mess" as Susan turned and saw what Dave was doing. "Well they just won't jump up into your hands, you know they're kind of shy" Dave winked as he raised a handful of dirt and worms in Susan's direction.

Just then into the store strode Mickey with Jim behind. Establishments such as the general store would not allow Indians such as Jim into their premises without a white escort. Even though Jim was young he understood the times and the times weren't a changing soon. "Lets get this show on the road" as Mickey deftly slapped Dave's arm. The dirt and the worms flew up in the air as Mickey put himself between Susan and Dave. He imagined himself to be the chivalrous lord who protects the fair maiden from the clutches of the evil and slow witted thief.

Bob, the owner, called for an attendant to get a broom and pan for the mess. "Just thought she needed help" Mickey answered as he laughed, turned around to Susan and started to flex his muscles. He knew that she would blush but also understood girls secretly loved the bravado of boys. "Since we all seem to be here now" Susan observed "daylights a wasting, lets get a move on."

Outside the back door at Bob's farm market there began a winding trail that proceeded about a 100 yards down to the valley floor. Jim brought along his dog, a mixed black mutt he named Sparky and led us down the trail. The journey seemed a little livelier with the dog in front. This trail paralleled the stream that eventually would lead to a large pond, it's dimensions being about 300 feet wide by 200 feet long. A line of trees ran adjacent to the stream and then around the pond.

The multitude of sights and sounds from Mother Nature drove Sparky from one side to another. Jim would let him have fun but when he wanted Sparky on the trail all he did was whistle and the dog was back on the trail. As we got nearer the large pond the stream seamed to slow down its motion. It somehow knew that the end of the line was straight ahead and there was nothing that could be done. Sparky was the first at the pond and put all his paws in the water and lapped up a little too. Jim was not too far behind with Mickey, Susan and Dave a few yards further. Many childish giggles could be heard as they played with the fishing pole like it was a sword. "En garde, I will protect thee fair maiden from the evil that is Dave" chortles Mickey as he tries to appear very muscular with a short fishing pole. "You'll have to do much better than that to scare me" responds Dave as he readies a counterpoise to Mickey. One funnier still because Dave is tall and gangly. "When will you two ever grow up!" Susan says as her eyes roll and she crosses her arms. "Just having a little fun, what's the big deal? Mickey asks as he slowly deflates to normal size again. "She's probably right" Dave says as he points to an area across the spot where they were at. "I think that would be a good spot to catch a few big ones."

As they continued to hike down to the pond the dog abruptly stopped. Jim also felt something was wrong. He knelt down to pat the dog and reassure him as he also looked in the same direction as the dog. He waited to speak until Dave, Mickey and Susan caught up with him. "Something in the air tells me there is danger behind us" Jim excitedly states. "What do you think it might be?" Dave asks while Mickey and Susan squint behind him. "Could be bears" retorts Mickey "but fear not, for I shall fight them off and save everyone" looking towards Susan, withdrawing a hunting knife. Looking at the knife Dave slyly says "That little knife will just piss the bear off." "I sure don't remember any bears in this area."

Susan and Jim chuckled at Dave's response but Mickey was embarrassed. He threw Dave an icy grimace, Mickey always wanted to seem strong in Susan's eyes. Jim stated rather forcefully for a young kid "We should head to higher ground because whatever it is its bigger than a bear."

Dave saw the worry in Jim's face and being the oldest felt responsible for everyone to return safely home. "I think we should all move to higher ground" Dave states "just to be careful." Mickey, seeming hurt, asks "What about our fishing? Who made you the boss? I'm going fishing no matter what you say!"

Dave could see that Mickey with arms folded was going to stand his ground. Why couldn't younger brothers just listen to their older brothers, especially in times of danger? Dave really could not remember a time when Mickey obeyed him. Since Susan entered the picture he seemed to be even more difficult to control. "Jim, take Susan and your dog to higher ground. Mickey and myself will continue to the fishing hole by the pond" Dave almost commands "If you see anything out of the ordinary give us a holler and we'll scram to high ground also." "I don't like us splitting up" Jim said "and I have a bad feeling about this one." "Don't worry so much" quipped Mickey "and when did Indians go so soft?"

Dave could see that Jim got really angry over Mickey's suggestion he was a coward. Before Jim could start with clenched fists toward Mickey, Dave got between them. He secretly wanted Jim to put a hurt on Mickey but thought better about keeping the peace in this situation. He motioned to Jim to begin taking Susan and the dog to higher ground and turned his attention to Mickey.

Dave could still observe Jim, Susan and the dog as they climbed up. The hilltop gave a commanding sweeping view of the valley below. Jim could still see Dave and Mickey as they meandered down the trail to the ponds fishing hole. Jim also tried to quiet his dog who was now barking and yelping. It's ears pricked up and looking back in the direction of the valley's beginning, the dog sensed some kind of impending danger.

After calming his dog down Jim was looking in the same direction. His senses were not as keen as the dog's but his gut told him that something was not right. He could barely still see Dave and Mickey on the trail but was ready to yell and signal the best he could when it became necessary. And it would become necessary very, very shortly.

CHAPTER 2

A Major Flood

Unbeknown to many people in the area, the Colorado River a day earlier had overtopped a levee. The levees were designed by the Southern California Land Trust Co. to stop any floods of the river. Flaws of design and underestimating Mother Nature would soon lead to tragedy. The river was engulfing and destroying everything in its path since the breach. Valuable farmland, livestock and small communities lay in the path of the Colorado River charting a new course for its riverbed.

Dave and Mickey were almost to the fishing hole of the pond when Dave noticed the stream leading to the pond getting wider every few seconds. Not paying attention Mickey ran with his fishing pole to the pond. Thinking this odd Dave looked up to near the top of the hill for Jim. Jim was waving frantically and pointing to the opposite direction where the start of the valley began. Dave could not see the town but could hear a slow thunder rolling their way. The stream getting bigger meant a flood might be coming their way. Emmitville was right in the path of a raging flood; trees, boulders, fences, parts of buildings, even animals became part of the rampaging water. Dave could see Jim, Susan and the dog climbing ever higher and he was glad they were safe. He knew it would be at the pond soon so he and Mickey would need to climb fast to avoid the fast approaching danger.

Turning to Mickey, Dave hurriedly commanded "We must get out of here quick and start climbing, a flood is coming this way!" Mickey unbelieving said "And leave all these fish here, you've got to be kidding." Dave pointed at the stream getting bigger "We do not have much time. You can stay and die with your fish or come with me and live to fish another day!" Mickey saw the stream getting much bigger seemingly every few seconds. "I guess you are right big brother but I would have caught the largest fish to show Susan who is the best!"

Dave rolled his eyes as he and Mickey began to sprint and climb as fast as they could. A sound like a fast moving freight train Dave surmised was the rushing water getting closer. Mickey and himself would have to climb extremely fast to avoid the onrushing flood. Elevation wise they were below the town of Emmitville and since water flows to it's lowest point, staying put was not an option. As they climbed, with Dave looking back in the towns direction, he noticed a tremendous wall of water cascading down from Bob's farm market. At this rate the floodwaters would merge with the pond soon and both of them would be in grave danger. He frantically urged Mickey to climb higher and faster as all around him like in slow motion familiar landscape was disappearing under the water.

As they were still climbing the hill Jim and Susan looked back at what was the town of Emmitville. The rampaging river was surrounding and dislodging seemingly everything in its path. The only road through town was gone and many storefronts were under water, some completely washed away. Susan was starting to cry and Jim did his best to console her but even he knew that Dave's and Mickey's chances were slim. The rapidly rising water, the swiftness and the sheer volume of everything dislodged and moving downstream meant disaster for anything in it's path. They rested on a large boulder once they finally got to the top of the hill, still transfixed by the sight of destruction below them.

Dave and Mickey continued to scramble through bushes, small trees and over rocks. Out of the corner of his eyes Dave saw a ridgeline, which was an old wagon trail. "Let's try and make it up there" Dave shouted and pointed as the roar got louder "so we can see what's coming" "Just get me out of here" Mickey responded "and I won't tell Mom and Dad you forced me down here to fish as I wanted to go to high ground."

Dave could not believe what he just heard but this was no time to argue. They could hear the crackling and rumbling of topsoil and trees being upended and churned like with a plow, only much faster. This brownish, muckish mass mixed with rocks, bushes, trees, lumber, even dead animals, moved like gigantic fingers across the valley. Dave and Mickey just happened to stay a smidgen ahead of the unraveling calamity but not for long.

Dave had reached the ridgeline first, pivoted and thrust his hand out for Mickey to grab. Mickey's outstretched hand touched Dave's when a tree limb came out of the depths and tore into Mickey's right leg. Mickey cried out in pain, Dave strained to hold on as the current pulled Mickey under for a short time. Dave now had both hands around Mickey's wrist. Pulling with all his might he was able to drag both Mickey and the tree limb to the ridgeline. Dave took out his hunting knife Dad had given him for a birthday present and began to forcefully cut the limb in two. Dave threw the severed tree limb down into the water, which was now closer than he remembered a few moments ago.

Acting faster out of pure adrenaline and terror he pulled out the ends of the limb that did not go through and hoisted Mickey a little farther. As Mickey was crying out in pain Dave heard above him the reassuring voice of Jim who had climbed down the hill to help his friend. Jim tore off his shirt and wrapped it around Mickey's wounded leg to help stop the bleeding. They both took a shoulder, got Mickey to his feet and proceeded quickly up the ridgeline, not once looking back. Hearing the roar of the flood subsiding they knew some distance was being put between them and the deadly flood. Both of them let out a sigh of relief when they saw Susan and the dog still on the rock ahead of them.

Susan attended to Mickey's wound as Dave and Jim rested upon the rock. What had seemed like a terrible dream as Dave opened his eyes became an eerie reality as he scanned the horizon. The town of Emmitville was mostly gone, only a few sturdy concrete buildings remained and they were slowly disappearing. As far as the farms that spread out from the town, every one was gone and submerged under a torrent of water. Dave did not want to think about his parents likely demise and turned to see how the others were faring. Even though Mickey was in pain he was kind of smiling because Susan was attending to his wound and calming him. Dave turned to Jim who was petting his dog and also surveying the scene. "Never seen anything as destructive as this before" Dave said to Jim "Just hope our parents are alive although looking at this" pointing in exasperation "I fear the worst has happened to everyone." "I think you are right" Jim answered "We were very lucky to escape. Mickey should be alright, maybe a limp for some time. I'm worried about Susan, she was trembling the whole time and if her parents died, she'll be a mess." "I'll look after her as much as I can" Dave sighed "We'll have to stay here on the high ground for a while, in a little while there should be some rescue boats looking for survivors. Until then, let's all keep warm and wait this out." Jim agreed and they all rested on the large boulder with Dave keeping one eye open and looking at the flood level. Dave and Jim surveyed the land and the flood water entering the valley. Since the valley was miles wide the rampaging river was filling it up like a big bowl of soup. What they did not know was that their valley was higher up in elevation than other valleys and towns down south. This meant the flood, brown with tons of topsoil and clogged in spots with all sorts of debris, would not rise much and just continue south, the new downstream.

As they waited and watched the destructive Colorado River cut a new course through the valley, worry sat in. After the initial danger and adrenaline rush had subsided, Susan, Dave and Jim openly expressed worry for their parents. "Do you think our parents or anyone in town survived that flood" Susan asked as tears welled up in her eyes. "I hope so" Dave responded reassuringly. "People should be searching for us soon but it might take a while."

As Jim scanned the almost under water valley he said "Dave's right, it might take till the morning until we get any help." Pulling out a few sticks of beef jerky from his pouch he handed them to the others. "Did not know how long we would be gone so I brought many of these."

Dave and Susan thanked him for thinking ahead as they were getting mighty hungry. Mickey was in and out of consciousness so Susan attended to his needs. Night time was coming soon so they all hunkered down on top of the large boulder. Dave and Jim agreed to take two hour watches looking for any rescue or rising flood waters. Way off in the distance Dave thought he heard a humming sound. Since he could not see anything in the pitch black he went back to much needed sleep.

As night gave way to the morning light the floods devastation became apparent. There was no town of Emmitville anymore as far as Dave and Jim could see. Everything seemed to be under water except for a couple of roof spires. Dave recognized these as the church and the towns hotel. They were both on higher ground but they did not escape the flood either. In the distance they saw what appeared to be a small boat heading in circles like it was looking for something.

Jim instantly got up, started hooping and hollering. Dave also started jumping up, waving his arms in hope of attracting attention. They could see the boat stopping, then turning in their direction. Susan and Mickey were awake by now with all the commotion and they were getting excited that finally some help was on the way. All around hugs went out and they drew a sigh of relief, their nightmare was over. As they sat back on the boulder waiting for rescue the physical and emotional toll of what had happened yesterday began to creep in. They sat there silent or a while, looking over once a fruitful and bountiful valley under water and eerily silent.

As the boat got closer the three men inside helped them aboard. They were careful with Mickey as he was still in pain; joy turned slowly to worry and apprehension. Thankful they were alive their thoughts drifted soon to those who probably did not make it. Still being kids they had hope maybe their parents were alive still, to think otherwise was a nightmare that never ended. The men covered them in blankets and left the boulder. It had provided an island of safety and they started on a new course looking for other survivors.

The news was not good. The rescuers told them that only a few survivors were found and they were badly injured. The mothers of

Susan and Dave were alive but their fathers were swept out with the floods. Dave decided to take his mother and brother Mickey, once they were in better health to their uncles farm in central California. An aunt of Susan's who taught school in southern Utah invited them both to stay with her once the mother felt better. Jim decided to go back to his reservation in northern Arizona since much of this valley would be underwater for a long time.

◇◇

The Southern Pacific Railroad finally tamed the Colorado River 18 months later but not before it created the Salton Sea.

◇◇

Years were passing. Mickey did develop a limp after several months of initial healing. The doctors said it would last probably his entire life which made Mickey angry. As they grew into young men Dave and Mickey had many arguments develop on the farm. In many of these Dave would accuse Mickey of shirking his duties. Mickey's injury was long ago and Dave thought Mickey was just milking it to get out of work. Dave's mother and uncle had enough of this bickering and thought religion might help.

Father Michael of the local parish ran a school for troubled boys and young men. Initially Mickey took to the Father and the school. Dave thought it was because he got out of farm work but talks with Father Michael eased his pain. For a while. Anger just got the best of him one day and he pulled a knife on some boys making fun of his limp. Seriously cutting them he decided was old enough and soon took off to southern Nevada.

Hearing about a small town called Las Vegas, a wild west railroad stop to Los Angeles, the allure of starting fresh and making a name for himself became a priority. His angry demeanor since the injury was completely opposite of his brother Dave. Thankful for a second chance at life after the flood, Dave threw himself into farming. He loved learning new techniques about farming and irrigation. His uncle saw this and offered to pay for him to go to college. Dave applied and was accepted at Stanford where he studied engineering. The course was challenging but Dave was doing well which made his mother very proud.

War clouds were rising overseas and enveloping most of the nations of the world. America kept out of it militarily but helped its Allies with vast quantities of supplies and materials. For many years it worked well this way until Germany sank an ocean liner with many Americans aboard. Patriotism surged and young men came in droves to enlist and fight. Tell the enemy the Yanks are coming to finish this once and for all.

CHAPTER 3

War, Remembrance and the Marines—1918

Along with the other young men across the country Dave enlisted at the college recruitment center. His engineering background while at school gave him the opportunity to become an officer. The Army needed engineers because this war had stalled into a defensive one. Battling from trenches and dug in gun emplacements, losses of men and material was appalling. Ever so slowly new trenches and emplacements were needed and engineers were required to build them.

Since the ports for shipping the men overseas were on the east coast most of the initial boot camp training was also close by. Congress had authorized tens of thousands of new slots for the Army and a few thousand for the Marines. The peacetime armed forces in America were very thin and not sufficiently trained for war. Months would be required to train and equip this new force for the fiery furnace of war overseas. This fresh transfusion of American men and materials would help the Allies eventually but time and acclimation to the fight cast delay and doubt among many foreigners.

The boot camp training molded various farm and city boys into men whose single purpose was to obey orders and destroy the enemy. The Army emphasized mass firepower into a certain objective whereas the Marines strove to give the individual more leeway to achieve this. This meant more marksmanship training with the weapon to make every bullet count to make the Marines a more lethal weapon. This meant a couple more weeks in training but this added training would pay off once the shooting started.

Dave had graduated top of his class in college and also was near the top of his military engineering class. The Army would give him lieutenant bars and he was to lead an engineer company. All his men were eager to leave for overseas duty in the war. They were told at the separation harbor to wait three days for a Marine company finishing training. As they waited Dave stood in amazement at the scene of the harbor. Thousands of military men loading ships as untold quantities of war supplies gathered and loaded in other ships. Never had he dreamed or seen such a spectacle before him. The might of America raised a patriotic fervor all round the harbor.

As Dave surveyed the impressive scene in front of him a company of neatly dressed Marines were turning the corner. As they marched in crisp unison one could sense the discipline and uniqueness of these troops. The men seemed more muscular and their movements more concise than anything Dave saw in the Army. They halted in front of the transport ship and after a few commands boarded it in columns. Most of the other men in Dave's command also viewed the Marines as they came on board. The last marine was Dave's friend Jim, years had past since they last saw each other but Dave yelled and waved. Once they found each other they hugged briefly and tried to find some space on deck to talk. Impressed by his gait and demeanor Dave said "So you bought that few, proud saying and now you are ready for anything!." "After this training" Jim looked back at his fellow Marines "I feel like I can do anything and not fear anybody." "You probably did not have far to go in that category" Dave smiled. "Have you heard anything from Susan, I've lost track of her." "She has written me a few times" Jim responded "Last I heard she became a nurse for the Red Cross when this war began." "Wouldn't it be something if we all could meet overseas and go over old times" Dave wondered. "Why didn't you write her?" Jim asked. "She told me she liked you even though Mickey seemed to get more of her attention." Looking another direction "Where is your brother and did he get over the accident?" A little embarrassed Dave said "I don't know, being young I guess I never picked up her feelings toward me." Shifting his feet a couple of times he began again "Mom, Mickey and myself relocated to my uncles farm in central California. Mickey left as soon as he got better to a small town in southern Nevada. Las Vegas I hear but I have not heard from him since. He still has a limp from the accident!." "Too bad" Jim responded with a small twinkling in his eye. "Just helped my folks on the reservation, followed the news sometimes and when America entered the war, me and a few buddies joined." "We wanted the toughest and special, the Marines seemed the part and here we are!"

Dave nodded and pointed to a marine sergeant who seemed to be in charge although a few officers were around him. Jim acknowledged Dave and told him "That's Gunnery Sergeant Greg Conner, former policeman from Chicago and tough as nails! A very good man to have on your side." Dave thought that since the ship would take a few days to get to France he should introduce himself. In war one never knew when they would meet again but to have a good man on your side was always a plus. Jim and Dave headed below deck as the loud speaker announced "chow is being served" as most servicemen headed that way too. Nothing like a free meal to get the men moving.

Behind the mess counter a Pvt. Nate Clemens was serving potatoes and mixed vegetables to the army and marines. Dave told Jim that Nate cooked for his engineer company while they trained and he was very good. Jim extended his hand and thanked Nate for the good food. Nate was black and Jim being a Navajo Indian they seemed to like each other from the get go. The officers and enlisted men kept separated at chow and their talk consisted mostly of what was ahead of them. A few newspapers were around and the men caught up with the most recent developments of the war overseas.

The transport ship was one of several that left the port, part of a convoy of destroyers, frigates and supply ships bound for England and France. The voyage was mostly mundane and the course kept well south of the north Atlantic where German U-Boats roamed. This made the trip longer but safer for the troops who would have to entertain themselves. The officers mostly looked the other way to let the enlisted men blow off some steam during times not spent training. Craps, poker and various card games abounded in bunk areas below deck, sometimes arguments and fights broke out between the men. Security was provided by the marines, their long history provided the Navy with police on board a ship. Of course, the marines gave wide latitude to other marines so the army personnel usually ended up with the short end.

Dave found out what his brother Mickey was doing in a round about way. He was introduced to a Lt. James Pescone who was in charge of the recreation and social services for the army unit he was attached to. "Lt. Dave Stanley, Army Engineer Company, pleased to meet you" Dave said while extending a hand to shake. "Lt. James Pescone, Recreation/Social Services Company. Your last name is Stanley, any relation to a Mickey Stanley?" "He's my brother, have not heard from him in quite a while. Do you know where he is?" Dave asked. "He's doing quite well in Las Vegas, owns a few businesses and is well known around town" James replied with a little grin.

Dave was glad he was okay but he knew his brother and that little grin on James face probably meant not the usual business. "Could you tell me a little more about my brother and his business?" Dave inquired. "He likes to be called Mick now," James bluntly said "he mostly has small gambling houses and a couple of lending businesses."

Dave was impressed by the seemingly successful business ventures although the tone of James answers bothered him. He politely exited the conversation when he saw gunnery sergeant Greg Conner enter the room. He wanted to converse with him because his engineer unit had been assigned to Greg's marine company. It also was advantageous because in the short period of talking with James, Dave's gut feeling said he was not a good man. As he made his way near Greg he looked back momentarily in James direction. A big man, not a soldier was whispering something to him and looking directly at Dave and the gunnery sergeant. Dave thought nothing of it but was glad to get away from James. Could not put his finger on it but there was something else going on. His mom would say give a wide berth to those kind of people.

Extending his hand Dave said "My name is Lt. Dave Stanley, army engineer and my unit has been attached to your marine company. Pleased to meet you, have heard some good things about you from my old friend Jim Foxsom." "Tough but nice young Indian" Greg said as they shook hands "gunnery sergeant Greg Conner at your service. Jim enlisted with a few of his Indian friends in my marine company shortly after America declared war. They stay together, look out for each other a lot but finer soldiers I have not found.

Great scouts, their Indian ways will help us in battle", Greg trailed off almost as if imagining it in his mind. "Do you know that officer over there?" as Dave pointed. "He seems legit but there's something that I don't like about him, can't put my finger on it though!" Greg looked in the direction and frowned. "Have not met him but I am keeping an eye on him. Some of my men say he is harassing them at card games for more money."

Dave nodded and thought a run in between the two hopefully would not occur. He actually would pity the man who drew the ire of a marine gunnery sergeant. They were tough men who did not mince words, if they did not like you, you were in deep trouble. Dave even felt better. He knew as long as Greg was keeping an eye on this guy he would keep away from his men. Greg and Dave said goodbye and would keep in touch now that their units would train and fight together.

As the trans Atlantic voyage continued the men were getting restless. The officers did the best they could to keep the men busy. Training and familiarity with the weapons and tactics of this war kept he attention of many. Greg Conner the gunnery sergeant always wanted more training for his men but also knew they needed down time also. He kept an eagle eye out for Lt. Pescone, his police intuition told him the guy was crooked as a bent stick. One night before they reached the debarkation port in France Greg almost came to blows with the lieutenant. It seems a few of his fellow marines came to him to complain about almost being jacked up. A big civilian man with Lt. Pescone asked forcefully for more money. When a marine lost at cards the house said this card game was different and the payout more. Greg and a couple of the marines who complained were walking towards Lt. Pescone and his large civilian friend. Both men saw fire in Greg's eyes and realized they might not get out of this unscathed so they moved quickly to the nearest exit. Greg hastened his walk and deftly signaled a couple of marine MP's to block the door. Frustrated, Lt. Pescone and his friend turned the other way and were ready to respond to the gunnery sergeant when a alarm went off.

A ship in the outer perimeter of the convoy had sighted a submarine and a general quarters alarm went out to all the ships. This meant that all non essential troops went back to their bunks below decks and put on life jackets. With the confusion and swiftness of the men to reach safety, Greg decided to pursue this issue another time. Tense hours passed as now the men knew they were at war. The shelling and explosions in the distance were proof that this was life and death. In the early dawn the all clear was given. As the men went up on deck the first sightings of land and the French harbor could be seen. A triumphant shout rose from almost every ship as the long journey was over. No one knew the length of the next journey, the war itself but many hoped it would be a short one.

CHAPTER 4

France and the Past

S cuttlebutt from last nights alarm about enemy submarines proved accurate. Two submarines were eventually sunk but not before they torpedoed two freighters. One eventually sank with great loss of supplies and crew; the other was badly damaged but still afloat. As rescue efforts began for that ship the rest of the convoy was still largely intact thanks to the U. S. Navy. The Marines and Army commanders were pleased with this help but knew their men were chomping at the bit to fight in this war. We were to be called the Allied Expeditionary Force (AEF) but some of the marines renamed it the Allied Execution Force because they were part of it.

As men and materials were being unloaded from the transports, orders came for their units and frustrated the commanders more. It seemed that the English and French who had fought and died in massive numbers under the enemies wrath were unsure of the Americans leadership. For months and months the American troops got more training in weapons and tactics of the Allies but they watched the war from the sidelines. Boredom began to set in. Sergeants and officers in charge tried to remedy this by giving R&R (rest and relaxation) to as many men as they could. This was also done in rotation so as to have some companies ready to go to the front on a moments notice. Many men used these 48 hour passes to visit the countryside and small towns scattered across western France. They did not know it at the time but many of them would not survive this war. France would be their final resting place.

It was beautiful countryside; rolling hills and farms it seemed as far as the eye could see, seemingly untouched by war. Postcard small cottages in groups with usually a center church steeple outlined a small town. Every day it seemed a farmers market was selling different fruits and vegetables. The various smells would tempt many an American farm boy with thoughts of home. A portion of these marines and army personnel were from the country. They put their passes to good use remembering past life on the farm. As these were mostly young men in uniform they looked for more adventure. This usually included searching for young French women. They enjoyed the wine from many vineyards and gambling from games of chance, mostly card games. It was usual to see Lt. Pescone along with his large civilian friend visiting these various places of R&R. As the men came back from their passes to their units they traded stories and more complaints about Lt. Pescone were surfacing.

When Dave heard these stories from his men he decided to check with gunny (gunnery sergeant) Greg for confirmation. Greg's men also told about the same stories. With Lt. Pescone not too far away the civilian man would corner a young enlisted man and forcefully ask for more money, all going towards the unit's fund. Cornered and alone, most would pay up but a few refused. A sharp, quick blow to the stomach usually would convince them to fork over a few more dollars. Sometimes more convincing was needed.

Dave could not believe an officer was behind this and asked Greg to accompany him. Members of Greg's marine unit were on pass and he wanted to ask them what exactly was going on. Dave and Greg took a jeep to a picturesque little town a few miles away. Word was a large house on the outskirts of the town was where the action was and drew many of the enlisted men. Men in wartime needed diversions and Dave just wanted to be sure this was being done on the up and up. Greg wanted another shot at those guys also because his gut said their actions were definitely shady if not illegal.

As they both entered the house they almost did a double take. Like a saloon from the wild west the inside was full of tables with various card games, even a roulette wheel. Enlisted men sat and stood around the tables as young French women in barely there nightgowns teased and drank with them. A bar with large mirrors behind it and a multitude of bottles in front reflected the action going on. Every once in a while a woman would lead a young enlisted soldier up the stairs as other couples laughing came down. Dave even thought he saw a few officers who he had met before on ship at the tables and coming up and down the stairs. Greg knew immediately what was going on; in Chicago he had busted a few brothels that were operating illegally in that city. Dave was intrigued by all this but had a sense this was not by the book and should not be condoned, especially by officers.

As Greg and Dave surveyed the scene a few Indian marines could be seen. They were huddled in a semi circle around an immense man in a suit and tie. Greg recognized Jim as one of the Indians around the big man. Their conversation, even for this noisy place, was drawing attention from the other military members around the tables. Greg leaned over so Dave could hear him. "I think we both should investigate that (looking towards Jim and the large civilian man). Other marines in my company say that a large man is always around when they cough up more money for certain transactions."

Dave agreed and replied "I wonder if there is a connection between him and Lt. Pescone?" Greg muttered as they started to walk "Yeah, like good cop, bad cop. I've seen this play out many times before."

As they got nearer the heated conversation both parties simmered down when the Indians saw who was approaching. They were silent, obeying the unwritten rule that you only talk when gunny asks you to. They did not recognize the officer with him but even more courtesy would be shown to him because of his rank. The big man met the steely gaze of Greg and like pit bulls their eyes were locked in, trying to sense weakness. Dave sensed the macho match going on and decided to talk first to try to cool things down. "I've heard from fellow soldiers that they must fork over more money here when they lose at card games."

Dave swept his eyes from the marines to the big man. "Any response why this might be so?"

The large man answered Dave but kept an eye on Greg because he felt uneasy around him. "We offer services to the men at a fair price. Most of the profit is going back into the décor and amenities you see here" spreading his massive arms around the room. Greg responded rather quickly "Fair price?, I hear different. Men in my company say they feel pressured to cough up more money. Sounds like a shakedown to me; I'm a former cop and I've seen a few!"

A former cop, now the large man knew why he did not like him. Feeling like he was in a box the large man began to sweat when suddenly he saw Lt. Pescone across the room. Lt. Pescone had already signaled three other rather gruff looking men to assist the large man. Upon seeing Dave he motioned him to join him at a his table to explain things. Greg saw the men coming his way and proceeded to tell Jim and his Indian friends to get ready for whatever. The men just encircled them but did nothing as if waiting for a signal. Like in the wild west it was a showdown and the other men and tables around them backed away. The tension was high but controlled, how long this would last nobody knew.

As Dave got to Lt. Pescones table there were shouts outside and a half dozen MP's (military police) entered the house. Dave thought they came to shut the place down. Lt. Pescone thought they had finally caught him in his illegal gig. They were both wrong. They were bringing news about orders for both the engineering unit and the marine company to join the front lines. The Allies needed help because the Germans were pushing towards Paris.

Glad that they were finally getting a chance to fight the enemy, most of the men hurried outside to trucks ready to take them back. Greg and the Indians eyeballed the civilian men for quite a while before Greg told them also to get into the trucks outside. Greg ambled up to the large man in suit and tie and said "This is not over, I'll be back!" got his hat and motioned to Dave to join him outside. Before Dave left the house he turned back to see all the men gathering around Lt. Pescone smiling and slapping each other on the back. He thought if he ever got the chance again he would just let Greg and those Indians loose on those guys.

As the transport trucks lumbered down the road the marines and army personnel sang songs. Most of the songs were ribald and for the young men some ears were hearing them for the first time. Miles wore on and as the convoy got closer to their billeting areas one marine then all marines started to sing "From The Halls of Montezuma." All kidding suddenly stopped. Even some of the army soldiers listened and joined in as the marines were glad to share the words and lyrics. It was as though the men were feeling for the first time the heavy, final seriousness of the moment in front of them. The marines wanted to prove to the doubting English and French commanders their true mettle under fire. Months of waiting and training, understanding the weapons and tactics of this war would prove invaluable at the front lines. Each man was alone with his own thoughts as to how would they perform as a soldier when the time came.

The journey to the front lines from where they were staying was a little over 7 miles. The drivers of the trucks had noticed the poor conditions of the road as they got closer to their destination. The men in the trucks saw more and more people walking the other direction looking ragged and forlorn. Carrying and dragging most of their possessions, their faces showed the strain and dejection of 4 years of ravaging war. Gone were the smiles and the laughter the men had known before. It was replaced with a sense of hopelessness about what the future held.

About a mile from the billeting area there was a Red Cross field hospital. Dave wanted to visit and talk to some of the patients plus there was a small chance that he might again see Susan. He had heard she was a nurse for the Red Cross and had volunteered when the Americans entered the war in 1917. The English and the French were taking the brunt of this war for the better part of 4 years. Their losses and those of the enemy were staggering, the fighting was mostly defensive. Miles and miles of trenches scarred the countryside. Going up and over with little protection between themselves and the enemy was pretty fruitless. Little ground was gained and these trenches bred disease as men lived and died in them. The elements, constant artillery bombardment, poison gas, rats and horrible living conditions almost made the sick enviable of the dead. Dave also wanted to gain some knowledge about his enemy; how they fought and what might be their weaknesses.

Dave leaned over in the jeep to talk with Greg. "Greg, I want to stop here and talk to some of the troops. You go ahead and get your men settled. Send a jeep back this way in an hour, I should be done by then" Dave said while motioning his company sergeant. "I could loan you a marine for protection if you want" Greg responded as he looked back at the convoy every so often. "It's a hospital, I should be safe but thanks anyway!" Dave answered, not wanting Greg to know he was looking for Susan. "1 hour and no more. We are close to the front and could be called up anytime, don't need to be caught with our pants down." Greg winked as the jeep sped away to catch the convoy.

As Dave entered the large hospital tent he could see that they really needed a bigger place for the wounded. Every little space was taken by soldiers in various degrees of pain suffered in this conflict. Doctors and nurses hovered over certain beds, looking at charts and adjusting tubes and machines as rounds were made. Some of the men were bandaged pretty good but some displayed horrible wounds from battle. Dave wanted to believe this was the war to end all wars as some politicians claimed. Sadly he thought this would not be the last.

One American soldier was receiving care and Dave went to talk with him after the nurses administered to his wounds. He was surprised to learn his wounds (broken arm, bruises up and down his body) were not from a skirmish with the enemy but at a local house used to entertain the men. Dave listened as the young soldier described exactly the place and the men him and Greg had visited not long ago. The young man had also overheard a conversation between the officer and a large civilian man. He was sure he heard Las Vegas mentioned sometime and Dave hoped that his brother Mickey wasn't involved. Dave thanked the soldier, wished him good luck, turned and suddenly looked into eyes so familiar. It was Susan who was just coming on her shift and she was just as surprised as Dave.

The intervening years were kind as Susan smiled and then hugged Dave. Emotions came welling up and they both teared up, knowing the time was short and wishing the circumstances were better. "You look so beautiful, like an angel amid all this war and destruction" Dave said as his eyes took all of her in. "Thank you but look at you, all big and confident in that spiffy uniform. You must have several women vying for your attention!" "Only wanted yours and now destiny will part us again" Dave was surprised at his honesty. "I'll ask the head nurse for 10 minutes so we can talk privately out back." "My jeep will be here soon but I would like that immensely."

There was a little patch of green near a tree not too far from the tent. Holding on to each other at the waist they proceeded down the path talking and reminiscing along the way. As they sat down and looked into each others eyes the urgency of the moment became apparent. The first kiss was tentative but it unleashed passions both were unaware of. They held and stroked each other for the longest time. It was as if time had stood still and Dave had dreamed of this moment forever. Dave looked down at Susan whose lovely face was aglow with an ease he had never seen. Seeing his jeep from a distance he knew the time was short to say what he really wanted to Susan. "I have not been this happy for a long time and when this is over..." Dave wanted to say more but Susan interrupted. "Lets live for right now and now I feel loved" as Susan closed her eyes, parting her lips for another kiss.

As Dave bent his face to hers he heard an eerie, screeching sound that seemed to get louder. Any veteran of this war knew this sound as incoming artillery but Dave was unsure what the sound might be. An errant shell from the enemy was about to explode a mere 25 feet from the tree Dave and Susan were at. For some instinctual reason Dave draped his arms and body over Susan's a split second before the blast. The explosions shock wave knocked Dave against the tree, he felt himself go limp and unconscious moments later. He learned later in the same hospital he visited that Jim the Indian had helped him and Susan back to safety. Dave also learned that Susan had suffered a bad concussion and was showing signs of total memory loss. Jim told Dave that doctors were sending him stateside for his wounds and Susan would probably be sent back too. "Tell Greg wish I was there with you all fighting the enemy. Take care of yourself and I hope to see you all down the line" Dave trailed off as the drugs were taking effect. As Jim stroked his forehead he said a Navajo saying which in English meant "Brothers forever, be strong!."

CHAPTER 5

The Marines

Jim started back to the billeting area once the doctors confirmed Dave's condition. Serious shrapnel and chemical burns would be sending Dave home to the states for rehabilitation. Doctors also told Jim that Susan suffered a bad concussion and lost most of her memory. It was sad they both were injured badly but glad they were both alive. Maybe in the future under better circumstances they would all meet again. Of course Jim thought this highly unlikely but fate brought them overseas together after 13 years apart, who knew what lay ahead?

After the convoy had delivered the troops, the army and marines were separated into respective companies. The commander of the army engineers was told of Dave's injuries and a new lieutenant was given his duties. The Germans were mounting an offensive and just routing the English and French allies. Hasty new orders came down from command and for the first time in the war the Americans would be on the front lines. The English and French generals were skeptical and hesitant about the American leadership but their backs were against the wall. The army engineers were still under foreign leadership but the marines were given latitude to have them fight under marine command. This made Greg and all the other non coms and officers very proud and confident.

Specifically the engineers were tasked with building trench lines ahead of the enemy for a last ditch defensive stand. This line would be studded with mines in front, miles of barb wire, gun and mortar emplacements to trap the enemy. The French and British guns and troops were to assist the marines wherever needed. Good communication was absolutely essential but it was confusing early on. If the Germans broke through the American lines, very little stood between them and Paris and possibly the end of the war. The Americans knew the serious nature of the next battle and the marines were anxious to prove their mettle.

The high command said the Germans would be in the area in 3 days which was not much time to build all the defensive positions. Work around the clock by the engineers and the troops was more than adequate to stop and hopefully repel an attack. Greg made sure his marines were ready with plenty of ammunition, good gas masks, bayonets, water, dry socks and uniforms for an extended period. As the marines marched to the front lines their spirits were upbeat as they remembered all their training from boot camp to overseas. War was the tests of all tests, the marines did not like a defensive battle but knew the world was watching. They did not want to let the folks back home be disappointed so they dreamed of heroic acts. Many were not aware that they would give the ultimate sacrifice and never return and see their folks back home.

It rained buckets as they waited for the enemy's approach. Living in a trench with hundreds of other men for days under relentless rain was not for the weak. Disease amid the unsanitary conditions took a toll on the men and the aid stations were kept busy. Training was even more urgent as the hours were dwindling down to a final confrontation with the enemy. The marines were given orders to hold the line, repel the enemy and after this was accomplished to counterattack in force. It felt like the British and French were saying to them "Take Charge and lead us to Victory." It was similar to a red cape in front of a bull. To a man the marines were happy to oblige this offer.

Night passed slowly by before the dawn of the third day as anticipation grew towards a battle that might decide the war. Intelligence confirmed that the weather was also hampering the enemy's advance by a day or two. The troops were ready for a fight but some of them thanked Mother Nature for slowing the inevitable. Letters were written to loved ones back home, for a moment it brought tears and relief to many a young soldier. When one is aware that this might be the last time to communicate with loved ones, thinking and emotions become clearer. But to the older marines this was their job and all in a days work. To other troops the marines over trained on marksmanship and making every bullet count. Overwhelming firepower on a target was the usual response in this war up to now. The marines would prove that deadly accuracy with a rifle could frighten even the toughest of men.

The weather was lifting so the English commanders challenged the Americans to a game of rugby. It was a light hearted attempt to heighten morale and lift spirits before a pivotal battle and it worked. It was the French and English against the Americans. Since rugby was like American football with some minor differences, participation in it was easy. Greg volunteered to coach the Americans and after a first half of rousing play they were only behind by 15 points. Greg purposely left Jim and his Indian buddies out of the first half. He wanted them to learn the game but also by keeping them out gave a false sense of confidence to the other team. Greg saw the Indians play a pick up football game with other marines during basic training. Jim was a punishing running back as his Indian buddies expertly blocked for him. As the Americans came from behind and soon led in scoring, the bewilderment on the face of the opposing French coach was priceless. The raucous roar from the marines as they counted down the last seconds was to Greg the motivational spark he was searching for.

Just as the game ended a siren blared. The men froze for an instant but then commands from the sergeants and officers had them quickly gather their gear. Making sure they had everything because this was for real they double timed to their posts on the front lines. Adrenaline was flowing not only from the game just played but in preparation of what was to come. Intelligence had reported that a massive wave of German men and materials were headed straight towards us.

Our French and British allies told us what to expect in battle, their experience made us listen concisely. Greg went up and down the trench checking his men and offering assurances they would fight well. A couple of reporters attached to the unit told Greg the whole world was watching the marines. Greg thought to himself "Fine, we'll give them a hell of a show!"

As the Allies took up their defensive positions in the trenches and behind with fortified gun plus artillery positions the enemy advanced. Through binoculars the German commanders could see the vast array of men and guns pitted against them. They were confident because of their earlier successes in routing the English and French in earlier battles. Intelligence told them that it was too soon to expect the Americans would fight plus they were untested and should be routed easily also. They miscalculated in at least two fatal ways; these were U. S. Marines and the French and British had a surprise. They had four Army battalions attacking both their flanks in conjunction with the first shot fired at this battle. Of course this all depended on good communication and coordination which up to now had been suspect. It was a good plan but in the fog of war anything could happen.

Just as the English and French predicted the Germans started with a massive artillery salvo. Gas shells were interspersed for the maximum shock value. The Americans trained extensively with all models of gas masks and seemed to prefer the British. Donning their masks and hunkering down in the trenches, the marines were experiencing the horrors of this war for the first time. A few forgot their training and in a panic rose and tore off their masks to breathe freely. They succumbed to the fumes or got hit with shrapnel from the incoming artillery and the medics worked on them. Greg was sure they were not any marines in his company to do this. He put the fear of God in them if they screwed up. The Allies responded with artillery in kind and also fired many gas shells to hopefully unnerve the enemy also. It seemed like a long time but the artillery barrage lasted only 15 minutes. The damage on both sides was substantial. Hundreds of men were wounded or incapacitated by gas or explosions and the aid stations behind the lines were already becoming close to full.

As the bombardment drew to a close the marines and the allies got their first chance to look over their trenches and spot the enemy.

Of course one just had to listen and thousands of German war cries emanated it seemed like at the same time. They were quickly advancing in columns, hoping to sweep the trenches and the guns behind in a massive rush. From behind the allied lines came a second round of artillery and machine gun fire. Scores of Germans fell but they kept advancing which made Greg say "Marines, we're in for a battle!." Greg and the allies were waiting for the Germans to lay down covering fire as their troops advanced. They were all surprised when little came. Under sporadic artillery fire more marines and allied soldiers crept up and looked over the top of the trenches. They saw the Germans advancing still but in less numbers and slower because of the defenses in front of them.

The Allied flanking battalions had timed their attacks perfectly (which was a rarity) and caught the Germans flat footed. Most of their artillery and some reserve units meant for the fight ahead turned 90 degrees to fight advancing forces. This slowdown of German might to the front lines gave the Allies and the marines breathing space. The commanders took advantage of this window of opportunity and gave the order to "go over the top." Greg, itching for his marines to be one of the first over ordered "Fix bayonets." Some of the marines were already taking deadly aimed potshots at the enemy and paused long enough to attach their bayonets. Countless hours of bayonet training for the marines made the bayonet a deadly extension of their rifles. It was like a spear backed up by bullets.

Greg, climbing above the trench looked back and commanded "C'mon and get up, you sons of bitches, who wants to live forever." Leading his marine company forward in three waves constantly firing Greg was confident they could rout the enemy. The deadly accuracy of the marines with rifle and bayonet led some captured Germans to nickname us "Tuefulhunden" or "Devil Dogs." The landscape was pretty much bare of any cover which gave no advantage to either attacker or defender. Scores of Germans and Allies died that day but the marines kept pressing on. With the marines at the tip of the spear they would slow down as the Allies on either side would catch up in line. As new ground was gained the mortars and artillery would move forward a little and shell the enemy anew. This tactic was taking a heavy toll on the Germans and Greg could see many men retreating to the rear. Confident of their initial success the marines wondered if anything could stop them. Over a small hill the marines saw a wooded area the Germans were retreating into. Greg wanted to press the attack but the Allied commanders ordered all companies to halt while they assessed the situation. It also gave the marines time to rest and recoup a little before the next battle.

Unbeknownst to the Allies the Germans were setting a trap in the event of the battle not going their way. A small forest, which used to be a rich land owners hunting preserve was behind the German lines. On both sides were small towns and hilly terrain. The Germans kept a lot of troops in both towns and in the former hunting preserve even more. No more than 200 yards long and 300 yards wide it did not look very formidable but once inside it was different. Tall trees rooted in a sloping bowl that included narrow ravines and boulders the size of houses gave the Germans plenty of defensive cover. A thick underbrush hid many a position of men and snipers also hid in the trees. Machine gun positions were triangulated to give maximum fire cover to the others. In this steel trap mines were placed every 10 yards or so to hinder any attacker with thoughts of forward or flanking advances. The Germans hoped to lure the Allies into this place if they had to retreat. A battle here would wear down the Allies and give the Germans the time they needed for a counterattack.

CHAPTER 6

Prelude To The Battle

The Allies front was extending about 2000 yards horizontally and communication between the units was very difficult. Jim and his Indian buddies were more important as runners between units to ensure correct orders were received. As the mass of Allied soldiers chased the enemy over a ridge new orders came down. The whole offensive was to stop. What Greg and the others saw ahead was a wooded area flanked by two small towns. They were at different angles 1-2 miles from the woods. Allied intelligence knew very little about this area, the French maps were confusing so High Command decided to stop. They could see the enemy retreating but they were not sure how many were just digging in for another fight. Now the runners had to gather the intelligence about the areas ahead without much cover. A dangerous assignment that would most likely lead to death or capture.

Greg was glad they stopped and thought about this next phase when all of a sudden he saw on both sides of him men advancing. A French general had ordered his men to advance and keep the enemy running. Greg had not gotten the order and was glad the marines were in this arena independent as a fighting force finally. Greg and the others watched as the French soldiers got to within a couple hundred yards of the woods.

Maybe the enemy was retreating in force but then all hell seemed to let loose. From every tree and every bush in the woods it seemed like an endless stream of fire went out to the French. It was not a greeting so much as an ending. The ending of any life in front of the murderous volley. The first line of French soldiers, the entire French line of about 75 soldiers just fell. None got back up. Those in the proceeding lines behind immediately hit the ground but it offered only a few seconds of safety. The enemy adjusted their fire and peppered the ground with copious amounts of lead and small mortar fire.

The Allies tried to cover any still alive French soldier with mortar and artillery fire directly into the woods. The remaining troops fired in the direction of the woods but their rifles were out of range. Most saved their ammunition in fear of hitting any surviving member of the French company in front of them. All efforts seemed to be in vain because the same amount of fire seemed to be coming out of the woods. The artillery fire into the woods was having little effect except for pruning the tops of the trees. The enemy on the ground was mostly undisturbed. The Allies for the most part watched as the brave French soldiers tried desperately to retreat. Howls of anguish as bullets smashed into body parts were heard above the continuous hellish fire from the woods. The fortunate soldiers behind their dug in positions were mostly silent and cursing. Many cursed their impotence to help a fellow soldier and some cursed cause this was war.

Greg cursed the stupidity of attacking a force without an adequate artillery barrage to hopefully lessen their numbers first. He would make it clear to those in marine higher command that without artillery first, the lives of his men in his company were not to be risked. In war you take risks but calculated ones. This insane charge made him mad that good men were lost needlessly without proper planning.

Just a handful of French soldiers made it back to the Allied lines. Their wounds were so grave that the medics gave them little chance of survival. Dusk was approaching. The days initial rout of the enemy had bogged down and a protracted fight seemed ahead. The engineer company Dave would have been in charge of fortified and dug deeper trenches and gun positions. Several days wore on as the Allies probed for a German weakness on all sides of the woods. This only led to big casualty losses by the Allies and it seemed they were at a stalemate. The Allied flanking battalions that won the initial battle were also bogged down. The lack of communication and coordination meant the small towns were still the enemies. The situation did not look good.

In his gut Greg felt that if the woods and the surrounding towns were not taken quickly a potent counter offensive could still take Paris. Greg's plan which he made known to the marine generals was for the marines to take the woods. The English and French Allies would flank the woods on both sides and attack the towns. With excellent timing and communication the other Allied battalions would join the fight for the towns and then join the fight from the rear of the woods. Before all this happened a 15 minute barrage from every Allied artillery gun into the woods and then into the towns would proceed. Greg was surprised when word came down that the generals, even the French and the British, liked and approved the plan. With Allied intelligence saying a German counter offensive was forming speed was of the essence.

For his plan to work Greg needed excellent communication and coordination. The record for these both coming together in this fog of war once the battle started was not good. What gave him hope was that the marines were finally an independent fighting force in this war. Being on the same page greatly enhanced the chances of success. Over several days he saw the results of many unsuccessful attempts to take the woods flounder. Greg knew the marines could take the woods but not without great loss of life. The enemy was getting stronger and intelligence reports reported numerous reinforcements arriving in possibly 3 days. The battle had to be soon and it had to be a knockout.

Greg gathered Jim and his Navajo friends. "Jim, we must know the enemies strength and the lay of the land inside the woods. Take the best platoon you deem fit plus your Indian friends, gather good intelligence and come back. If you must kill do it without drawing too much attention to yourselves. You have 18 hours before the main attack begins, good luck and Semper Fi!."

Jim checked his watch, nodded and shook Greg's hand. After picking out 8 of the best marines to accompany him with his 4 Indian friends they left to formulate a plan. Divided into 3 teams carrying grenades, a pistol and knife, they would under the cover of darkness sprint and low crawl to the woods. Entering the front, left and right sides would give them a good idea of how the woods looked inside. Jim fashioned extra moccasin or cloth soles around the shoes of everybody for a quieter advance. A last check of ammunition and watches as they waited for nightfall to arrive. At the agreed upon time they split up into three teams and advanced into what the men were calling the Valley of Death.

The stench was almost unbearable. Dead soldiers were left rotting where they fell because it was too dangerous to retrieve them. They advanced together for about 50 yards and then split up again, one team going right and the other left.

Silently they closed the distance between them and the woods. The last 25 yards or so they low crawled very slowly to the edge of the woods and then quickly over. No movement from the Germans, luck and Indian skill were working together.

Jim and his team quietly crept down a small ravine lined with underbrush on both sides. He decided they would get a little rest there before daybreak. A large boulder almost the size of a small house looked like a perfect place for this rest. Even though they heard many German voices and movement above them, getting some shut eye was relatively peaceful. As day broke Jim and his team, after a couple swigs of water and beef jerky pieces, set out. All the teams knew they only had a few hours to gather intelligence on the enemy in the woods. At 1100 hours the Allies would begin an artillery barrage of the woods and surrounding towns. The shelling would last 15 minutes, hopefully weakening the enemy and providing cover for the escaping marines.

Greg wanted to maximize the teams chances of survival. He got permission from his commanders to advance 3 platoons of sharpshooters and machine gunners. They were to advance 100 yards, fan out left and right to cover the teams of marines from the woods. Twenty minutes till 1100 these platoons set out quietly hugging the ground to get into position. Some marines covered their noses with cloth to avoid smelling the rotting corpses but some could not help but throw up. After they found some high ground they set up their machine guns and waited for the artillery to begin. Greg had also got the artillery batteries to agree to fire smoke shells at the edges of the woods. This would obscure the area in between the Allies lines and the woods which was mostly barren of defensive positions.

Jim and his team had advanced slowly inside the woods. Sketching gun emplacements, estimating troop strength, he was amazed at how well organized the defenses were. His gut said this was planned, he even saw snipers in some trees well stocked and comfortable. Checking his watch and signaling his men to withdraw to a pre designated point, they carefully reversed direction. They waited near the point where a few hours earlier they entered the woods. Jim hoped his friends leading the 2 other teams were safe and doing the same.

As 1100 hrs approached Jim heard movement behind him. Many German troops were moving down the tree line to take up positions for a possible assault. All the marines silently drew their knives and put the other hand around the pistol handle. Jim saw a single German soldier stop and point in the direction of one of his companions. As he alerted other soldiers Jim pulled a pin and lobbed a grenade toward the unsuspecting enemy. Firing and throwing his knife into a German soldier Jim could only hope for the shelling to start soon. The other marines pistols found enemy flesh and before they could reload the first shells landed. It exploded in the midst of the German soldiers, killing many instantly and dazing others nearby. Jim wasted no time as he lead his marine team quickly out of the woods, hastily zigzagging back to the Allied line.

The woods were now receiving the brunt of the shelling but the surrounding towns received a fair share also. The front of the woods received smoke and continuing fire from the special marksmen and machine gunners Greg had sent out earlier. All this helped confuse the enemy. They hunkered down, every once and while firing blindly ahead as they awaited the charge of infantry. One of these errant shots did find a marine in Jim's team. He heard the cry and doubled back, hoisting the wounded marine across his massive shoulders. He heard friendly voices urging him on so he headed quickly to them. As he got to his fellow marines cheers went up around him. Two medics put the wounded soldier on a stretcher and back they went to the aid station. Jim stayed with the other marines to give cover to the other 2 teams that were still out there. Until they were safe Jim would not leave a marine behind, an oath all marines believed in.

The other Indian friends of Jim arrived almost at the same time but from different directions. One team had lost 1 marine due to machinegun fire, the other lost 2 marines due to mine explosives. They were all headed back to the Allied lines when German artillery suddenly rained down upon them. They quickened their pace and were glad when they heard familiar American voices shouting "Get the lead out... C'mon!." No one seemed happier than Greg who whisked the members of the team away quickly to a big tent. Officers were inside ready to find out how strong was the enemy in the woods so they could plan the attack. Greg had snuck in some whiskey for the marines for their bravery. The next few hours would require a few stiff drinks.

CHAPTER 7

The Battle

The officers and top sergeants of the Allies met in a big tent to discuss the battle plans. Jim and his fellow Indian friends discussed what they saw in the woods. Even though the artillery bombardment was heavy little damage was done. The tops of the trees were mostly gone but the Germans were dug in pretty good, like ticks. Jim also said there were plenty of them in machine gun nests and defensive positions around natural cover. Some snipers were in the trees but how many would survive the next salvo was unclear. "In your estimation could an attack from three sides like your scouts did be successful?" Greg asked. "I think coming in the side and the front doors could confuse the Germans enough" Jim responded while officers listened intently.

The artillery officers said they had enough shells for another 15 minute bombardment but needed rearming very soon. A call went over the wires for a convoy of trucks to bring more artillery soon. As they did not know when these supplies might arrive the Allies were vulnerable for a while. Without the big guns they would just have to rely on the individual soldier to win this battle. The English and French were not as confident as the marines in this strategy. They wanted big guns backing them up but the marines were different. Their whole training emphasized the individual soldier and the havoc they could cause.

It was agreed that the marines would attack the woods and the French and British would attack the towns. A 15 minute bombardment of both the woods and the towns would proceed this attack. The English and French soldiers would head out east and west 5 minutes before the barrage. There would be plenty of ground to cover before the towns came into sight.

Hopefully all this artillery would keep the Germans hugging the earth to give the Allies time to advance. Greg thought his marines could cover a little over 200 yards during the shelling. After it stopped another 100 yards would still be needed to reach the woods. Without much cover a lot of his men would be killed in this charge. Greg and his marine officers wanted smoke shells like before to be used when they rushed the enemy. The marine artillery battery said they had some but probably only 3 minutes worth. This was agreed to and Greg knew it was better than nothing. It was agreed to begin the initial fusillade at 3am to take advantage of darkness and the early morning fog.

All the marines now readied themselves for the battle to come. Guns were cleaned, ammunition checked and reserves loaded on belts. Grenades were clipped to empty spaces on the uniform, gas masks and entrenching tools also were carried. Camouflage was put on the the face and canteens were filled with water. This time soldiers and marines knew some of them would die here. The next few hours would be spent by some praying with some nervously looking out in the distance. No one wanted to die but to a man they did not want to let their fellow soldiers down. Success or failure depended on working as a team. The marines knew this but gave considerable latitude to the individual marine when things went bad. Adapt and overcome were going to used a lot here because when the fog of war appeared you just needed to push on.

Greg gathered his company of men in a small area behind the Allied line. He shook the hands of every marine, looked into their eyes and saw the courage behind them. He began to speak. "I've seen you through basic training and training overseas with our Allies. You are the best men I've ever been with and I am proud to lead you in battle. The enemy is strong and will be hard to dislodge from their dug in positions, but we are marines! In our proud history we have never been defeated and never will. I feel sorry for the enemy for they will soon feel our lead and bayonets. Our hands and fists will extinguish their lives so we can win this war and get back to our wives and girlfriends." A small roar of "Hoo Ha" went up and many smiles lit up among the men. "Get a few hours of sleep, be like steel in the morning and let's roll those bastards!." More muffled roars and lots of back slapping ensued as Greg shook more hands. He told Jim that he would like him and his two Indian friends to lead the assault. They would take the same routes used earlier for better success. Before they parted they shook hands and Jim said "Semper Fi, see you on the other side." Greg smiled and left to confer with other officers and top sergeants.

30 minutes before 3am the soldiers were awaken to a smell of hot cakes, eggs and bacon.

The engineer company lent Nate and a few other cooks to serve a hot meal before the battle. Some men wondered where all this good food came from but the majority just gulped it down. Thanking Nate and his cooks Greg proclaimed it the best he ever had under the circumstances. Nate laughed and offered the same meal once the marines had won the battle and everyone around smiled. The marines finished their meals and went back to get ready. Gear was double checked, plans memorized, prayers said by believers and non believers. The few minutes before the battle was started by the artillery was anxious for most men. Sifting into thoughts of life and death were past loves and loved ones. The British and French soldiers had departed in separate directions to attack the towns. The trenches held only marines but the Germans thought they were full of Allies. This deceptive beginning was working pretty good so far.

As soon as the artillery boomed their shells across to the woods and towns, Greg signaled Jim. Jim signaled his other 2 Indian friends and hundreds of marines began to move slowly across the Valley of Death. The woods and the towns were being lit up and pummeled so the marines moved a little faster. Greg wanted to get as close to the woods as possible before the artillery stopped. Many a marine had secured a cloth piece before they left as to not smell the rotting corpses of dead soldiers. Silence was essential even though the big shells were deafening. In between the fusillade the Germans were probably listening for a sneak attack.

Jim signaled his Indian friends to begin their journey east and west to enter the woods from the sides. Hundreds of marines followed them. Greg low crawled to a little knoll where he could see their progress. The glow from the exploding shells were extending a good fifty yards from the woods. This would be a good place to wait before the artillery stopped. Greg wished it was closer but they had to deal with it. He just hoped the other Indians and marines noticed this also.

Greg looked at his watch with a small flashlight. One minute to go before the barrage. He looked through some binoculars to the team on his left. They were in position and holding 50 or so yards from the woods. Now looking right he saw the other team advancing a little too close. Enemy machine guns and rifles opened up. Cursing to himself he now saw the smoke shells landing and exploding near the edge of the woods. Knowing the element of surprise was now gone, Greg signaled the other team by flare to attack. There were 300 men per line and three lines. Silently the word was passed down all three lines to fix bayonets. Greg shouted "C'mon you devil dogs, let's put these Huns out of their misery!" and led the charge.

Part of the plan Greg got approved was to attack in three waves. Greg led the first wave, Jim the second and an officer would lead the last one. Hopefully this leapfrogging plan would cover the remaining distance to the woods. Every minute for 3 minutes a new charge would begin until the artillery smoke stopped. Greg's marines had advanced twenty yards or so when a hail of bullets met them. The smoke screen was working fairly well so the Germans fired blindly in different directions and strait ahead. This indiscriminate shooting did find many a marine but many knew to hug the ground and keep low. The cries of "medic!" from fallen marines were heard but many just kept going. Low crawling over fallen dead soldiers from the previous battle was not fun. The alternative, getting up and running held risk of death from the machine guns that spewed death.

More firepower was added to Greg's line as Jim's second group of marines dodging bullets and aided by smoke arrived. As they inched there way up to the edge of the woods their individual marksmanship was having an effect. Some German guns were silenced but the machine guns were still taking good marines lives. Greg snagged Jim and a couple of excellent marine marksmen. "We have got to take out those machine gun nests" Greg said pointing. "We'll flank them and go down the line, take out as many as you can!." Crawling and running intermittingly they struggled until they reached one corner of the woods. They paused just for a few seconds and listened to the fight to their left. It seemed just as intense but Greg motioned the others take aim at a machine gun 10 yards in front. They fired and silenced the gun crew.

Individual German soldiers around the machine gun now turned around and fired. Greg took out a couple, Jim threw his knife into the neck of another and the others threw their hands up. Wanting to move quickly and destroy the enemy, Greg and Jim gathered the soldiers weapons. Put into a pile standing up, Jim rigged a grenade to them and they all exploded. Jim retrieved his knife from the soldiers neck, let out a war cry and the others fled.

As they continued down the forest edge killing and dislodging many Germans more marines were advancing. When they entered the forest sergeants, corporals or privates took charge depending on who was left. Marine training gave maximum responsibility to the individual soldier when upper chain of command was lost or dead. They would just have to figure it out themselves; unique in how men were used to fighting battles. What was a trickle became a flood as the last wave of marines charged. Entering from the side and gradually from the front the marines overwhelmed the remaining enemy. The front of the woods was secure but at a cost of hundreds of injured and dead. Greg told his men to form a line. Not knowing the progress of the other two groups he led his men down into the woods.

The last of the smoke shells were exploding. The two groups that attacked the sides were still not in the woods, resistance was heavy. As Greg's group made progress the Germans decided to reinforce the front of the woods. Unaware it was no longer theirs they sent every third man guarding the sides to the front. These Germans became casualties as soon as they entered the marines view as dawn approached. The carnage of the attack was apparent and ugly. At full strength now both groups of marines rushed the sides of the woods. Once inside the woods the majority of fighting was hand to hand, gruesome but advantageous for the marines. Bayonets met flesh, fists met cheek bones, the enemy never met a more deadly and unforgiving foe. As the enemy was routed and as agreed before the battle 3 platoons were left to guard the flanks. A make shift line was formed and the marines from both groups headed down to join their buddies in more fighting.

The shelling the night before finally did take a toll on the enemy. More explosives landed in the woods because the trees that protected the enemy before were mostly kindle. Even though they were well dug in major losses occurred in both men and material. Now with all three groups of marines converging down into the middle of the woods the defense was rattled. Greg sensed victory was near when he saw a multitude of Germans filtering in from behind. Where were they coming from? He thought quickly. The only side they did not attack was the back side. He thought the enemy might be using a path connected to the small towns for battle reserves. Apparently the British and the French were not hurting the Germans hard enough in the towns. Greg gathered Jim and his Indian friends. "Take 50 marines, hurry and go up the side of the woods, find that path and secure it. We'll join you when we mop up these guys" as Greg slapped the shoulder of Jim.

Jim signaled every 5th marine to join him. When he had 50 he led the group running parallel until they were at the edge of the woods. Another 50 yards to the corner where he rested and surveyed the area. He saw the path to the towns maybe 50 yards in front of him. Not wanting to expose his men he led them through the woods. Seeing only a couple of machine gun nests on either side of the path he signaled 10 marines. They would flank and attack the opposite machine gun while Jim attacked the other. Jim waited as they got in they got into position. He signaled the attack with a war whoop. The Germans were taken by surprise and those coming down the path were killed by commandeered machine guns. Jim and his marines then took up positions for a possible counterattack.

It never came because finally the British and the French aided by artillery were inflicting great losses. In the two towns near the woods the Allies were routing the Germans so much they were beginning to flee. Some diehard elements of the enemy refused to leave but the overwhelming numbers of the Allies made decisions easier. As the bulk of the Germans retreated north dusk was approaching. The French and British forces overtook the towns but did not forget the marines in the woods. Two companies of about 500 soldiers were dispatched to enter the woods and aid the marines. When Jim saw the Allies he thanked the Great Spirit in the sky for their timely entry. They turned and as one big unit headed down to help Greg, his friends and the marines. By the next morning all the Germans were either captured or killed. The woods was theirs but the marines suffered hundreds of casualties. As a fighting force they proved their worth and were respected in the battles to come. At home news of their exploits sold many a newspaper and radio coverage was worldwide. The Yanks were helping win the war and the marines were writing new chapters to a storied history.

Although this battle was fictional it is loosely based on one of the important battles of WW1. The battle of Belleau Wood would mark the beginning of the marines as a separate fighting force for America.

CHAPTER 8

1931 New Beginnings

The barren and dry lands of the southwest held a secret. If only a constant source of water supply could be found, bountiful crops could grow. Farmers knew this but in 1905 the uncontrolled Colorado River flooded for 18 months. Many lives were lost and great destruction ensued. Farmers wanted to build a huge dam for irrigation but had no money or expertise to accomplish such a task. They figured only the federal government would be able to tackle this endeavor. Of course they had there own problems. The stock market collapse of 1929 sent unemployment skyrocketing and many people lost nearly everything they had. Dave read in the newspapers where they were planning to build the world's largest dam in southern Nevada. There were quite a few people who thought it was a crazy idea in these difficult economic times.

Farming was difficult and not too profitable when money and demand was drying up. Dave reasoned and told his mother that he would seek a job building this dam. Dave also promised to look in on Mickey, now Mick, as per his mothers wishes. Dave saved his life many years ago but if Mick was turning to crime Dave would feel no pity. Being brothers of course he would always try to reach out to him. Sometimes he thought the distance between a good and bad man seemed like a chasm.

One of the most inhospitable places on earth, the Mohave Desert, was chosen to build the dam. For years geologists and engineers surveyed the canyons the Colorado River snaked through. The best site was in Black Canyon although Boulder Canyon was studied too. Many factors went into picking Black Canyon. Near the top of the list was it was not still in an earthquake zone and it was narrow. A more daunting canyon to build the world's largest dam in would be hard to find. Cliffs that rose 1000 vertical feet on both sides of the river. Temperatures in the summer that exceeded 130 degrees and no trees to block the cold wind in the winter. In this environment they wanted to corral and tame the here-to-fore untamable Colorado River. It led many people to believe they were crazy cause it had never been done before.

Dave had left his farm and mother for Las Vegas, a small railroad stop town on route to Los Angeles. Chosen to house the employment office, hundreds if not thousands of men lined up for a chance at work. Word had spread quickly throughout the country that work was available. Even before the ink dried on the law passed by Congress to build the dam, men and their families arrived. Like moths to a flame people were desperate for any work during what people were calling the Great Depression.

After a couple of days travel Dave disembarked from the train and lined up at the employment office. He would seek shelter later because hordes of men were in line awaiting any job opening. Most of the men had experience building other dams but some would experience difficult on the job training. One either learned to adapt and overcome for this job or you were out of a job. It was pretty black and white. Although Dave had no experience building dams his engineer education and military credentials served him well. He was hired as a general foreman whose initial task would be the hardest.

Six private companies would merge into one entity supervised by the government. Before they could do anything the river had to be turned. For centuries every spring the snow would melt at the tops of the Rockies. This tumultuous thaw would ultimately form a muddy and cascading river that flooded many areas. The fall and winter it would dry up to a trickle so the people demanded government action. The only possible way to turn the river from its ancient river bed was through the canyon walls. The plan was to build 4 tunnels, 2 on each side, each 4000 feet long to divert the river. One of the companies had expertise in tunnel building but this would push the envelope.

Dave left the employment office overjoyed he had landed a job in this economy. Walking down the line of men awaiting interviews he saw someone familiar. It was his old boyhood friend Jim. It was hard to miss him, he stood 6'2" and was still very muscular. He was in line with 3 of his Indian friends. As Dave approached and tried to sound serious "Hey, you there!" Jim turned around and smiled. As Dave hugged Jim and shook hands with his friends some men stared. Relations between races was still frowned upon these days but Dave did not care. He had not seen Jim in many years and had many questions to ask him. "Wait for us here, we are applying for the high scaler jobs" Jim said.

The high scaler position was not for the faint of heart. It consisted of repelling down the canyon walls and sitting on a bosun chair. A 44 pound jackhammer would be lowered down and one would drill a hole into the rock. Dynamite would then go into the hole. The high scaler would then swing away to a safe position and await the explosion. After the explosion they would swing back, loosen and chip out the remaining debris and start over again. This way the rock edges of the canyon could abut smoothly with the dam.

It took a special breed of men to undertake this job and Indians were suited well for it. Most had no fear of height and went on to help build skyscrapers in major cities. Jim and his friends got hired as high scalers and looked for Dave. The man doing the hiring needed them in the tunnels first. Jim would drive a truck hauling muck from the tunnels. Two of his friends would be nippers and one would be a chuck tender. Nippers would supply drilling crews with fresh drills, dynamite powder and water. A chuck tender would assist drillers on the drilling jumbo. A 5 ton Mack truck was layered to hold 30 drillers at different levels. The tunnels were drilled, dynamite was loaded into the holes, the jumbo reversed out of the tunnel. After the explosion the muck was removed by trucks and the jumbo returned for more drilling. Sounded easy enough but this would be the hardest task of the entire project.

The companies provided a bus to the work site from Las Vegas. All the men without families were going to be housed in a dorm not too far from the proposed dam. Men with families would stay along the river in tents, shacks, whatever could be rigged up. The companies knew this to be temporary until they could build a permanent work camp. The depth of the bad economic times drew thousands of desperate people to an unforgiving desert. Hope of a job gave people the strength to survive in these tough times. At 50 cents an hour for average pay the men felt very lucky for any job at the dam as Dave and Jim sat in the bus they tried to catch up on each others lives. Dave asked "I saw you last in WW1, what have you been doing since then?." Jim responded "Not much after the war, just farmed and did odd jobs on and off the reservation. Farming and jobs were hard to come by after the crash in 1929. We heard about the government plans to build the biggest dam in the world in southern Nevada. Myself and a few friends pooled some money together, got on a train and here we are!." Dave recalled the interview he just had for his job as foreman. Speaking to Jim and his friends "They probably will use you first in the diversion tunnels and then as high scalers. They have to turn the river first then excavate the rock for a smooth fit. Its pretty amazing that we are here together over all these years!, heard from anybody else?"

Jim knew who Dave meant but was reluctant to say anything about Susan for he heard only rumors. He and his friends checked out Las Vegas as they arrived 2 days before Dave. It was a rowdy town and not too many places let Indians in. One gambling hall did let them in although they had to stand in the back. Even though it was smoke filled and alcohol scented Jim recognized two people immediately.

From a distance he saw Susan arm in arm with Mickey, now Mick. She was stunning all glamoured up but something was not right about her. Her eyes, once she got closer seemed vacant. Even though she smiled at something Mickey said she seemed lifeless. She was not the Susan Jim remembered. How she got here and met Mick Jim wanted to find out.

Before Susan got injured word spread of this angel in the hospital. Lt. Pescone sent one of his men to check and he confirmed her loveliness.

After the injury it was arranged by Lt. Pescone that she would convalesce stateside in southern Nevada. Sums of money was exchanged and she was eventually brought to Mick.

Mick was aware that her condition would only get better with rest and relaxation. He did not want her to get better and remember her past life. His plan was to keep her busy and so she was with him constantly. He slowly introduced her over the years to booze, drugs and pimped her out to his wealthy friends. Her condition worsened and memories of anything before the injury were a blank. Mick knew memories of the past would be hard to come by if she was distracted enough. His plan was working beautifully.

Jim strode over to one of the bartenders who was washing some beer mugs. "Hey buddy can you tell me a little bit about that woman" as Jim nodded towards Susan. The bartender, eyeing Jim suspiciously said "That's Mick's woman, hands off if you want to live." Jim also saw 3 big men surrounding Mick and couple of them looked familiar. Jim could not remember where but he was sure he saw them somewhere before. "She has been here since the end of the war, she had a terrible accident and Mick took her in." He then leaned over and whispered carefully so only Jim could hear. "She sometimes entertains the big crime bosses who come here from out east, know what I mean." He winked as he said it, Jim acknowledged it but really wanted to punch him.

This was not the Susan he remembered and the injury during the war was probably behind the change. Being around Mick or Mickey if he was involved in crime didn't help either. Jim walked back to his Indian friends and they all decided to leave. As they all left they passed within a few feet of Susan, Mick and the big men. No expression from Susan but the men locked moderate stares at each other. He just could not place them but he felt his friends were trying to remember also. Jim vowed to keep the knowledge of Susan to himself for as long as he could. Assuming Dave's heart would break if he learned about her being with Mick all this time Jim said nothing. Jim knew eventually the beans might spill but they both needed focus for the big job ahead. The worlds biggest dam was going to be built and distractions were not needed at this point.

After a few seconds Jim responded. "No, have not heard from anybody else. Did you know a Greg Conner? He was my gunnery sergeant in the marines, saved my life more than once. Wish he could be with us here, he was a heck of a man!." Dave replied quickly "Got to know him pretty good, his marine company was attached to our Army engineer company. In a fight or back alley you want a man like him to cover your back." They both nodded in agreement.

As they watched the landscape change from small town to desert memories of the war were exchanged. "Do you remember that big house they turned into a gambling place in France?" Dave asked. Jim smiled and suddenly remembered where he saw those big men in Las Vegas before. Now everything kind of clicked and the link with Mick, Dave's brother, was even more in focus. "We all almost got into a big fight in that one" Jim said. They laughed for quite a while the bus made a left turn. The landscape changed even more as craggy igneous hills abounded on both sides of the road. The bus driver said they were a few miles from the site for the dam.

Everyone was looking out the windows of the bus as they descended into the bowels of the canyon. Volcanic rock abounded in every direction, it was devoid of any trees and most vegetation. Only when they could see the river was there a little green vegetation on the sides. A large three story wooden dorm built on the incline near the river came into view. The bus stopped and the newly hired workers departed, each gazing up at the canyon. The view was awesome as it was spellbinding, to think men could build a dam in this environment.

Bosses and foremen were lined up and already calling off names just like in the military. Groups of men went into the dorm basically with explicit instructions to be back in line in 10 minutes. Yep, hurry up and wait thought Dave and Jim as they found their bunks. This immense project would tax every man who worked in this canyon physically and emotionally. There was nothing here, nothing around but it was work and in times like these it would have to do. A paycheck is a paycheck Dave thought. For a few men the heat and hard work would prove to be too much.

Their work was grueling and as the summer months wore on many men died from heat exhaustion and stroke. Not only on the site but in the shack and tent groupings by the river that also claimed women and children. The companies knew they had to build a more permanent housing solution for the workers and their families. In August several men management thought were just rabble rousers turned out to be union leaders and sympathizers. They got most of the men in a lather about unsafe work conditions at the site plus low wage cuts. Every man walked off the job to strike but it only lasted a few days. Management had no trouble finding hired help during a depression. They also hired men with clubs, found the union leaders and sympathizers and drove them off the site.

The companies now knew they had to cordon off the site and probably the new city as well. They asked the government to declare the site a federal reservation with federal marshals and gates for entry. As the fall and winter months gave a little relief to this problem the companies found a solution. Beginning next year they would break ground on a city 7 miles from the worksite. The mass of men, some with families that came for a job demanded more than just a work camp. It was intended to be a model city without liquor or gambling. A clear head was needed for this unprecedented public-private enterprise. The city was to be called Boulder City in reference to the Boulder Canyon Project Act of 1928.

CHAPTER 9

1932 New City and the Colorado Tamed

The companies who were building the dam each had expertise in different phases of the project. A complete infrastructure of roads and railroad lines needed to be built to the dam site. Las Vegas was the nearest town and it was 40 plus miles away. The town at least had the Union Pacific Railroad as it was between Los Angeles and Salt Lake City. The government officials let it be known to the company executives that a separate town was needed. One that was closer to the site plus it was to be free of liquor and gambling. The companies found the ideal site 7 miles away from the site after several studies. Work quickly commenced to erect housing for the men who were now working at the project.

First teams of mules would grade the roads needed and in the desert a city was beginning to grow. The men and their families were anxious to leave their dilapidated dwellings near the river. The houses were going up so fast that some men got off work and could not find their home. When they entered what they thought was their home and found someone else there, many objects went a flying.

This model city for the workers would need a law enforcement presence. Calls went out from the government office in Las Vegas for federal marshals. Since most of them were still fighting Prohibition experienced men in law enforcement were next in line. In Chicago Sgt. Greg Conner of the police force volunteered for this new position. His captain put in a good word for him and he was ready for a new challenge anyway. He boarded the train headed eventually to Las Vegas but stopped along a few other western cities. As he gazed out the windows the changing panorama intrigued him like when he was a boy. He liked westerns and dreamed of being the sheriff of a wild west town. Standing up to the bad guys, bringing order and peace to a town was like apple pie. His dad was a policeman, grandfather too, maybe it was in his blood.

After a couple of days of travel he disembarked the train in downtown Las Vegas. Not much of a town as he scanned around but it sounded and looked the wild west part. Gun fire and boisterous hollering could be heard; were they sure they did not need him here? A thin man in a suit approached him and asked for identification. After shaking hands we got in a government Model T and headed out towards the site for the dam.

The hot emptiness of the desert became apparent as we traversed the bumpy dirt road. The man pointed out a railroad line being built to our left, seemingly going on for miles and miles. A flurry of activity was spotted once we got over a hill. A new city was sprouting out of the sand; the workers would relax in comfort now the man said. After we passed the gated checkpoint he took me to the companies head quarters and introduced me around. They made me chief federal marshal since I had the most experience and most military service. Word was this job was a veteran preference gig; could buddies from the war be here? This job sounded pretty demanding so the memories would have to wait.

About a week after Greg arrived via train two government workers disembarked and would begin work soon. Emma Blood would stay in the employment office in Las Vegas and she would assist in hiring the men. Although it was strictly forbidden for a government worker to favor any new hires she had a soft heart. Apparently she also had a soft heart for money and jewels which Mick would use to his advantage. She visited Mick's gambling house many times and quickly got into debt. Mick lavished her with money and jewels and when the time came blackmailed her. He would not tell her government supervisor about her behavior if she let a few of Mick's men inside. Mick wanted a few handpicked men in Boulder City and maybe the dam site as spies. He already had some contacts in the hills surrounding the city with bootleggers. They needed to know now with federal marshals on site when the coast was clear.

The other government employee was to be the city manager responsible for everything that went on in Boulder City. His name was Elijah Simp and a more straight laced individual would be hard to find. Did not smoke, did not drink, did not cuss; vices were unknown to him. Knew government policies inside and out and his word would become law in this new city. The government wanted to run a tight ship here because the job would depend on it. The country needed a positive economic lift during these times so nothing was left to chance. Protect the new city and make it a model for little could be done for the sloth and sin of Las Vegas.

Work on the diversion tunnels was progressing steadily and so was the infrastructure to the site. Railroad lines for supplies and roads to transport men and materials were being finished. Boulder City was taking shape and soon the workers who lived in the dorms along the river packed up their belongings. The married men and their families already had moved into small homes erected seemingly every day and night. Workers seemed happier on the job site once the housing became available. Management did change a few safety rules after the strike last summer but the pace and hard work continued. A friendly competition among the different shifts began; who could drill the farthest in 8 hour shifts. A distance of 46 horizontal feet was claimed by one shift and it would be pretty hard to beat.

When men succumbed to the heat in the tunnels they were packed in ice. Rushed to the hospital some made it and others did not. Medical knowledge grew to tackle this problem. Salt was added their water and some individuals only job was to carry and distribute it to the men. Deaths declined for this cause but other causes of death were not so easily solved. The men just kept their nose to the grindstone, relieved to have a job in his economy. If they gave up they knew other men in minutes would replace them so they hunkered down.

Dave and Jim were packing up some items in the dorm when the door flung open. The light obscured his face as he shouted "Hurry up men, who wants to live forever?." Instantly Jim knew that voice and rushed to the door, bear hugged Greg and let out a whoop. Dave was not sure who it was but as he came into the light Dave smiled. As Dave and Greg shook hands they could not believe that all three of them were together. "Good to see you after all these years, what have you been up to gunny?" Dave inquired. "I'll tell you on the truck, it's picking you and a few others up" Greg responded. Greg rounded up the other passengers and they all got on the truck for Boulder City. Greg, Jim and Dave sat near the front and Greg started to answer the last question.

"After the war I went back to Chicago and for a couple years sold insurance. Can you picture me selling insurance? Dave and Jim chuckled a little bit as Greg continued. "My dad, who was a beat cop, saw that I really wasn't happy and suggested applying to the police. I did and think that I found my true calling. Spent many years as a Sgt. during Prohibition chasing and fighting criminals dragging down the city. The biggest boss was Al Capone, a mean and smart sonofabitch, excuse my French. Just got tired when I heard they were looking for men experienced in law enforcement out west here. Always wanted to come out here so here I am!, now how did you both get out here?

Dave and then Jim recounted their stories to Greg as they drove along the hillsides to Boulder City. The journey was interrupted many times by machines and workers still building the road from Boulder City to the dam site. As they waited their stories continued amid back slapping and laughter. As the truck emptied out its passengers Greg said "Get off in an hour, how about meeting at the mess hall and we can talk some more." "Fine and I'm buying!" Jim responded as he smiled with Dave and headed towards their new home.

One day Jim just happened to look under the crawl space underneath their dorm building. There curled up in the shade was a dog, apparently there to get out of the hot sun. He asked several of the men and they did not know how the dog got there. Jim whistled and tried to signal the dog to come to him. The dog nipped at his hand so Jim went to the mess hall and brought back some pieces of meat. The dog came willingly this time and ate the pieces while Jim stroked his back and head. He showed others the dog who was friendly once you gave him something to eat. He named the dog Nip remembering the first encounter with him. Knowing it was against rules to keep a dog in the dorm he just took him to work. The workers liked having a dog around the site and he just roamed everywhere. If they had an extra sandwich more than once the dog got half.

The city was growing and transforming from seemingly cactus and mesquite bushes by construction seemingly 24 hrs. a day. The workforce would enjoy the amenities and relaxation of a small town 7 miles from the dam site. One of these amenities was a large dining hall built to feed the multitude of workers. It was called the Anderson mess hall because of the owners, the Anderson Brothers. For years they fed the great number of people employed by Hollywood in the entertainment business. The contract was awarded to them and many volunteered to go and feed the workers at this historic site.

One such fellow was Nate Turner who had been employed for many years as a cook. Management let him go also because a few white people recently had seen him preparing the food. It had closely guarded the secret that for many years a black man was cooking their food. Although California was not Alabama segregation of the races was still mostly adhered to. It did not really bother Nate as he was looking forward to a new location and challenges.

He was shown his new place of work but he could not live in Boulder City. The companies did provide him and a few other black men transportation to the site and the city. They ended up living close to the river like the families did before the city was built. It was hard but that was how it was. Put on night shift he did not know that Dave, Greg and Jim also were there. The men had all the food they wanted 3-6 times a day in contrast to the rest of the country. These were very lean times but the companies needed strong and able workmen. Many men stuffed their lunch boxes with as much food as they could cram in there. One built up an appetite with the difficult and demanding jobs they did.

As the summer gave way to fall interest was buzzing at the site. The tunnels were almost finished and the river could be tamed and rerouted. Two cofferdams were built, one up and downstream in 24 hours by continuously dumping rock from the tunnels. Thus a truck going across a trestle bridge would dump its load every 30 seconds. Cheers went up from the men. Big heavy gates were raised and men with shovels dug at the temporary dike around the entrance. The Colorado River slowly turned from its ancient bed and followed a new path through the diversion tunnels.

Now that the hardest part of the project was completed the company and government officials breathed a little easier. It would take months to dewater the site and get down to bedrock. Jim and his friends were told to change their jobs to high scalers. The canyon would now be pruned with dynamite and steel allowing a good fit between the dam and the rock. 1933 would start a new phase for the project. The country hoped to find a better direction with a new president.

CHAPTER 10

1933 Dam Rising

Boulder City forbid booze or gambling in city limits and was gated, so to speak, and guarded by federal marshals. The surrounding country side was vast and offered many ways to enter; albeit illegally. Mick and his partners in crime knew this and sent several men into the hills surrounding the city. Starting illegal stills to provide Las Vegas with liquor Mick also tried to plant men in the city. Any way he could disrupt the workers to spend their hard earned money in Las Vegas was fine by him. If the time came he wanted men on the ground there to help him in whatever he might plan. Federal marshal Greg Conner was kept busy and was concerned about this affecting the building of the dam.

One early summer morning he was called with Elijah to a downtown business that sold mostly woman's clothing. Since Boulder City was a company town the company paid the men in scrip accepted only at company stores. Three young ladies were there with the store manager. Greg and Elijah did not recognize these ladies as a couple of them reeked of too much perfume. The manager showed Greg and Elijah the scrip the ladies used to purchase dresses and some female items. Greg asked where they got this scrip and one of them said from several of the workers. Greg thought for a while and he knew the answer to his next question. He asked them what for, one said sheepishly "For services rendered." Elijah turned red, Greg made sure they had transportation back to Las Vegas. He did not know if Mick had a hand in this but he wouldn't be surprised.

Boulder City was a safe and decent place to relax after a grueling shift at the dam. Several men though craved more action and most anything occurred in Las Vegas. Drinking, gambling and interactions with loose women was the cities stock and trade. In an area called Block 16 men could interact with women for a price. The oldest profession, prostitution, would probably help build this dam. Greg was sure some workers looking for a good time didn't have real money so they used scrip. Greg saw the trouble inherent in this bartering system and alerted company officials. From now on real money was to be issued and the scrip fell out favor.

To be sure this did not occur again he would have to go to Block 16 and talk to the madam. While in Vegas why not talk to this Mick fellow also and warn him to keep away. Since he was Dave's brother why not bring Dave along and try the family tie thing. He did not want to spook Mick so maybe Jim and his Indian friends would be a good backup. Greg arranged all of them to meet at the mess hall around 6pm.

After the bedrock was exposed the engineers wanted to anchor the dam further. They were concerned water might seep under the dam and gradually dislodge it from below. A trench 50+ feet wide and 135 feet deep was dug and the first bucket of concrete poured June 6, 1933. The plan was to build the dam up in separate wooden blocks interconnected by vertical and horizontal grout joints. The chief engineer came up with an idea to cool the tremendous amount of concrete poured. A refrigeration plant built atop the lower cofferdam would pipe chilled water through 1 inch pipes laid horizontally every 5 feet. Dave was amazed at all the intricate engineering needed for this project. He was getting more of an education on the job that school could ever teach him. Greg called up and told him of his plans. Dave needed a break from the job plus he did tell his mother he would try and contact Mickey. He agreed to meet at the mess hall plus he would contact Jim and his friends.

At 5:45pm inside the mess hall Greg was having coffee waiting for the others to show up. Wanting to personally thank the cooks who fed his men at all hours he went in the back. Nate had subbed for a guy on day shift and was preparing to leave when Greg entered. It took a few seconds but they both extended a hearty handshake to one another. "It's Nate from the war and I still remember that good meal!" Greg said beaming. "You have a good memory, gunny, how the heck did you get here?" Nate answered back. "Long story and you won't believe who else is here. Remember Dave and Jim?" Greg asked as he slowly walked out to the front. "Sure do, man what's the odds of all of us being here?" Nate said as he hesitated. "We're not supposed to go out the front" Nate gestured to Greg.

Greg saw the uneasiness in his eyes. He also remembered in the war that the blacks fought well against the Germans. Society might have a problem but he respected Nate. Any man willing to lay his life on the line for another was okay by him. "Nonsense, come out here and let's wait for the others. How about going with us to Las Vegas to celebrate old times?" Greg said while checking his watch. "Sounds great but they won't let me in those gambling places!" Nate replied. Showing his badge and gun Greg said "I think they will when they see these!"

Coming in the front door was Dave with Jim and his Indian friends not too far behind. Dave could not believe that Nate was sitting with Greg laughing. Dave spent more time with Nate in his engineer company in the Army. Walking briskly he shook Nate's outstretched hand and could not believe that fate had brought them together again.

"Since we all are here I got two cars out front" Greg motioned "so let's get going, I know you guys need some sleep after a hard day. Dave, take Nate and one of Jim's friend and I'll take Jim and the others. Just follow me cause I'm stopping first at Block 16." All of them did a double take on that one. They had heard the stories about that place and thought it odd Greg was going there. They had a good laugh when Greg said it was official business.

After a bumpy ride across the mostly barren desert the two vehicles arrived in downtown Las Vegas. It was not very big but the main street was aglow with lights enticing newcomers to several gambling joints.

Greg led the way past these places to the a side dusty dirt road. At the very end were several shacks and a long wooden one. Young sultry ladies were lounging on chairs and some were not very modest. Jim, his friends and Nate stared out the windows like kids at a candy store. Dave parked near Greg and out of the corner of his eye looked around. It was a real place this Block 16 but Dave found it hard to believe some women lived like this. His memories of Susan were still intact and he did not want another woman.

Greg got out of his vehicle and turned to Dave and said "Won't be long. Just going to have a nice chat with the madam." Dave knew nothing about the situation and just stayed behind he wheel. A woman motioned to Nate with her finger to come over. Nate looked at Dave and Dave said "Not too long because Greg will be back soon." Nate was out the door quickly because it had been a long time without a female. The others stayed in their cars because they feared gunny would not approve. Some ladies came over but most stayed in the shade.

Greg was true to his word and did not take too much time talking with the madam. As he exited he saw Dave, Jim and his Indian friends in the two cars but no Nate. Walking up to Dave he asked "Where's Nate? I'm ready to go." Dave responded looking at one of the shacks "Guess he's taking care of business, said he wouldn't be long though." Greg headed towards the shack, sighing to himself but understanding human nature. From behind the shack he saw the back of an expensive car. He heard the door slam and it quickly sped away. Finding it odd he began to knock on the door when Nate appeared with shirt in hand. "Got to go, Nate, we have to visit another place before we leave" Greg said while looking around. "Sorry about that but she said she really liked me" Nate said looking down. "They say that to every customer" Greg chuckled as they both walked back to the cars.

On the main road again Greg saw the sign "Mick's Place" and parked in front. They all got out and Greg got them to gather around. "Just want to say this once. We are going inside, getting a table and having 1 or 2 drinks. You guys deserve the break from work, relax and let me do the talking. I want to talk with Mick and see if we can come to an understanding. Dave if you want to talk later with him, since he's your brother, go ahead. You are my guests this evening so let's have a good but sensible time!"

Heads nodding in agreement they turned and were about to enter the establishment when the doors flung open. Two big men were throwing out a smaller man onto the sidewalk. "Don't ever come back here or we'll really hurt you!" grumbled one of the big men. As they readjusted their suits they looked over to Greg and his party. The big man eyed Nate and said "no blackies allowed, do your business elsewhere!." Both men laughed but Greg put his hand on his hip, exposing both badge and gun. "I'm a federal marshal, we're on official business and we just want to wet our whistles" Greg intoned.

Greg only came up to chest high with them but a marine doesn't back down to anyone. The sight of the badge and the gun probably persuaded them to grudgingly let them in. Once inside they found an empty table and sat down to stares from some of the patrons. All kinds of games were being played with cards and at slot machines.

Greg had heard chatter from a back room and telephones ringing. It reminded him a lot about the illegal bookies back in Chicago he had arrested. Another place, another time but he would love to shut this place down. The bar was full with a good number of men standing around with drinks in hand. Some people actually left when they saw Nate and one of the big men noticed this. He proceeded up the stairs while the other big man folded his arms and glared at Nate.

A waiter approached nervously watching Nate. "What will you have?" he asked Greg who seemed to be the leader. "Beers all around" quipped a smiling Greg. "Except for you, we don't serve your kind in here!" the waiter shot back, pointing at Nate. Jim and his friends had this happen to them many times, still they were angry. Dave and Greg saw this and Greg looked over to the big man. The big man was smiling as he walked over to the waiter and whispered. "Beers all around" he said but you could tell he was not happy. A potential troubling incident avoided and Dave breathed a sigh of relief. Greg thanked his lucky stars also and hoped it lasted.

In a few minutes beers were served to everybody. It was like giving water to a thirsty man in a desert. Greg and Dave sipped theirs while

Jim, his friends and Nate almost gulped theirs. "Easy does it guys" Greg said patiently "One more round and make it last!." "Sorry about that, gunny" Jim said as he looked around. Other people in the gambling hall were eyeing the Indians and Nate suspiciously. "We're awful thirsty but we will behave ourselves."

Jim almost forgot where they were a then remembered a conversation with the barkeep two years ago. Susan wasn't herself and Mick would most certainly show her oft to humiliate Dave. Jim leaned over to talk a bit with Dave."You know your brother Mickey is here" Jim said as he watched the stairs. "Susan is also with Mickey who likes now to be called Mick. Susan has not been herself since the war accident you both shared. Don't believe everything you see, once she remembers she will come back to you." Jim went back to drinking his beer and felt better."Thank you but how long have you known about her?" Dave asked while trying to grasp it all.

A few seconds later Mick came down the stairs with Susan flanked by three big and gruff looking men. Dave locked eyes on Susan as she came down the stairs with Mick. Susan did not reciprocate his gaze but smiled and waved to friends she knew.

Jim, seeing the hurt in Dave's eyes waved at Susan and winked. Susan looked at Jim and then at Dave and smiled. Mick saw this and you would have thought someone poked him. He looked over to the big men and they surrounded Jim and his friends. Greg saw this and instantly said "C'mon fellers, he was just having fun" pointing at the beers. Jim slowly stood up and was level with the big man next to him. "I'm sorry but I thought I'd seen her someplace before. My fault" Jim said never taking his eyes off the big man. As they stared at each other Mick finally told all of his men to back off. Greg and Dave both drew a sigh of relief when it all calmed down.

Greg motioned Mick and Susan to sit down at the nearby table. The big men got a couple of good chairs and they both sat down. The big men were beside and behind them and the gambling hall returned to its noisy self. Greg leaned over and looked directly at Mick as Susan began puzzling over Dave's face. "I've been to Block 16 and had a nice chat with the madam" Greg said. Seems a couple of her women went to Boulder City and tried to buy clothes with workers scrip. I told her it was illegal to do and then I asked her if you had any connection with the women. She said no but I've been a policeman for many years; she was lying. I told her to stop it and now I'm telling you, be careful what you do in Boulder City!." Greg put one hand on his hip and uncovered his badge and gun for Mick to see.

The place got really quiet like it knew something might happen. Mick was slowly smiling and turned to Susan who still was trying to remember Dave's face. The smile quickly faded. He looked back at Greg when James 'Vinny' Pescone came down the stairs with a woman. They were laughing and then the woman caught sight of Nate at the table. She cast her eyes down and Vinny saw this. He then looked over to Nate and said "Don't worry honey, I'll protect you from that nigger!" Nate just smiled and maybe the beers gave him courage. "She told me that she likes big niggers in bed!" and then the fists started to fly.

Jim and his Indian friends went for the big men, Nate for Vinny and most of the gamblers went for the exit. Greg calmly sipped his beer while Mick and Dave stared at each other. The man to man fighting of the Indian marines left the big men hurting. Even for a cook Nate roughed up Vinny pretty good. Mick saw all this and told his men to stop and Greg did the same. Greg said "Let's go boys, our work is done here" and they all left, brushing themselves off. Mick looked over the damage to his men and ego and shouted "Next time you all are dead." Greg did not hear the dead part, only next time but he was sure that they would tangle again.

CHAPTER 11

Spring 1934 Bitten, Crushed and Buried

I nformation had been coming in to the marshal's office that there were a more union men on site getting workers riled up about safety precautions. The construction companies were aware of the rabble-rousers trying to halt work until these issues were addressed and fixed. Their ultimate plan was also to have the workers off the worksite to spend more time and money in Las Vegas. Mick had paid and planted these so called union men for his benefit, country be damned. Anytime he could also hurt his brother Dave in the process was a bonus gift. If he could pull this off the big bosses would have to take notice and he would go higher up in the organization. To leave this hot, dry, railroad stop of a city he took to new heights of vice wouldn't be bad either.

Being just a foreman Dave was instructed by his supervisor to inform the marshals to round up the union people for quick termination. Building this dam during the Great Depression was very fortuitous for the employer; with hundreds of men applying for a single job on the site they could let anyone go and have a replacement in minutes. Dave called marshal Greg Conner, his old war buddy and explained the situation. "Greg, how you been?" "We are having some problems here at the dam and in Boulder City with some union organizers."

Greg responded "Is it those guys again from the IWW?." "We think so and management wants them all rounded up and fired" Dave said. "We can not afford any job delays." "Just so you know we think Mick is also behind this" Greg went on. "In delaying the project he hopes to get more idle workers spending money in his establishments." "Thought he might be involved in this" Dave sighed. "Do what you have to do, I'll be here if you need me."

As Dave hung up the headache he had earlier in the morning seemed to be waning. With Greg on the job he knew it would be possible to concentrate his thoughts at the worksite. What Dave did not know was that his conversation on the phone was overheard by Emma Blood. As Dave left the room, Emma called Mick in Las Vegas and informed him of Dave's conversation with Greg. Mick wanted to teach Dave a lesson, maybe even slow down the worksite a little. He thanked Emma and sent two goons with trusted confidant James "Vinny" Pescone to make sure Dave would get the message. They made sure they took the back roads so as not to arouse suspicion from the marshals.

Emma went into a side room, away from her supervisor's gaze to call a couple of men. Mick told her to delay marshal Greg's arrival at the dam until his men could get in place. Emma told them to create a fracas in three separate parts of town. These incidents would bog down the police and give Mick's goons the time they needed to set a trap for marshal Greg at the dam site.

The bright yellow sun was just rising over the hills when the radio in Greg's car started to cackle wildly. Another sweltering summer day was ahead and these early activities pointed towards a busy day also. The incidents were a small bomb detonated near one of the double decker open air buses used for worker transport. Another one was an apparent robbery of one of the merchandise stores downtown in Boulder City. The final one contained shots fired at workers near the entrance to the federal reservation in Boulder City.

Initially Greg thought that some union agitators were behind the incidents but the shooting was another story. The union people had never used guns before so this incident was suspicious in nature. Greg decided to personally check out this occurrence but something did not jibe with the usual M.O. of the union activists. Directing the two other marshals to go and check out the other situations, he made his way to the entrance of the federal reservation called Bolder City. "What went on a few minutes ago out here, did anyone get hurt?" Greg asked as he lumbered out of his vehicle towards the policeman at the gate. "Several shots fired from over there in the desert" the policeman said as he pointed to where he thought they originated from." No injuries but a couple of shots hit the checkpoint shed and gate."

Greg looked at the bullet holes, then out to the desert and while scratching his head said to the policeman." Good job, keep your eyes peeled. Whoever it was might come back so be ready!" As he drove away he remembered Dave's conversation with him earlier that morning. Maybe these were just diversions to keep him away from the dam site where something big might be going down. With that thought his foot seemed to be a little heavier on the accelerator.

The dam site seemed to be abuzz with the constant activity of hundreds of men. To the casual observer it looked chaotic but it was organized chaos. Each man had a job to do and like worker bees contributed his part to the success of the whole. Dynamite was used to dislodge the tons of rock from the canyon for a smooth interface of the dam and power plant. A twisting road far from the actual dam site was provided to store and load the powder into the dynamite sticks. The job title for this task was a powder monkey although a cool head and nerves of steel should have required a more dignified title. This road was not guarded and Mick's men took advantage of this overlooked aspect at the construction site.

Mick's three ruffians drove down this road in a used beat up jalopy. They were looking for a good spot to lure and ambush marshal Greg. Many places to hide and spring a trap down the hilly and twisting road but their clothes (suits) would stick out like a sore thumb. Mick thought earlier about this problem, the burglary at clothing store would provide them with the basic work clothes used at the dam site. This should have blended them in well into the work force except that two of the thugs were over 300 lbs. Although they looked like Ned and the first reader, the men took opposite positions behind two large boulders on both sides of the road.

As Greg got close to this road an employee flagged him down. Seeing the unusual jalopy with the unfamiliar men inside he was concerned about what might be going on.

Greg asked "How many men do you think were in the car?" "About three, I think and they were big, ornery looking guys" he responded, motioning to where he last saw the vehicle.

In his vehicle Greg slowly proceeded down the road scanning the rocks for any movement. By this time he pretty much discounted any union involvement, his gut told him a more sinister hand was at work. Greg was aware of Mick's illegal operations in Las Vegas. Since he also was Dave's brother and hated everything the government and Dave were doing here, he became the prime suspect.

According to the worker at the top of the road Greg was looking for big guys. One of the aspects of the Great Depression were the very hard, lean times for most everyone.

A shortage of jobs and food led to the majority of people being thin. Greg's search was narrowed as most of the workers on the construction site followed this trend.

Another worker proceeded to get Greg's attention and Greg stopped the car. Happy to have allies in this fight, Greg was told that just around the corner two big men were hiding behind some rocks. "Did you see any weapons?" Greg asked, squinting because of the hot, desert sun "and anything about a third man?" "Sure I saw a machine gun and a shotgun carried by the two big guys" the worker said hurriedly. "The other guy who seemed to be in charge drove the vehicle a little further down the road, parked it, and seemed to be waiting for something."

Greg thanked him for his help and told him to leave for the dam site. Checking his own weapons, a shotgun and two revolvers, he loaded them fully and shoved any extra shells into his empty vest and side pockets. He decided to park his vehicle and move as quietly as he could down one side of the twisting road. His plan was to flush one man out while pinpointing the other position by basically firing first and seeing what they did.

The two thugs thought Greg was coming down the road in his car, the noise of which would give them plenty of heads up for an ambush. They were unaware Greg had been tipped off by some workers as to their whereabouts. The hot midday sun made waiting for the ambush particularly vexing for the two hoodlums. Being overweight did not help either as sweat was beginning to soak through their clothes. They were not accustomed to being this uncomfortable. Fear of Mick if he found out they were slacking on the job kept them somewhat semi-alert looking for marshal Greg.

Greg was silently creeping around some rocks when all of a sudden an ominous rattle sound was heard. He froze in place, knowing that rattlers were plentiful down this road. The rattler continued to coil and hiss, his rattle kept sounding warnings to keep away. Greg was well aware of the snakes deadly reputation, many dam workers were bitten, some seriously by the venomous devil. Although Greg froze when he heard the rattle, one of the roughnecks waiting in ambush did not and this gave Greg the ability to locate him and devise a plan to take him out. Greg also did not realize how close he had crept up to the first assassin. Unfamiliar to the sound of a rattler, the ruffian moved just slightly from behind a huge rock. Greg was 20 or so feet away when he saw the metal gleam of a large machine gun.

Knowing that he had the element of surprise he slowly pulled back the triggers on his shotgun. Unsnapping his side pistols, a quick bulrush with guns a blazing would silence one of them while giving him a good idea of the other's location. He would just have to take his chances with the snake but in all the commotion maybe it would be just as confused as the other guy. He took a deep breath, looked again at the path he would quickly take to the rock, said a silent prayer and took off.

Shotgun blasting first, he aimed it in the general direction of the huge rock, hoping for a lucky shot but just wanting to get the thugs attention. Greg zigged the opposite direction of the blast, correctly assuming that the bad guy would hunker behind the rock and return fire from the blast side. The assassin did not wait long to return fire, firing his machine gun around the rock where the blast came from. Greg was on the opposite side of the rock, trying not to breathe too heavy and give away his position when down the road Vinny saw the movements of marshal Greg in trying to kill one of his men. He yelled and motioned with his arms trying to alert both his men of the marshal's presence. A split second before the shooting started he did alert the other man with the machine gun on the opposite side of the road that something was amiss.

Greg had reloaded his shotgun and as soon as the machine gun blast stopped he pivoted around the rock a little until he saw the outline of the thug. The workers were right, he was a very big feller and Greg was glad he had the shotgun because the pistol would not be enough for this guy. As soon as Greg unloaded both barrels chest high at the ambusher machine gun bullets sprayed the front of the rock. A wounded yell from the side of the rock and a loud thud as his body hit the ground produced a little smile upon Greg's face. It was short lived as Greg tried to think of how to get in to position to kill the other assailant peppering the rock with machine gun fire. Plus the fact that he did not know where Vinny was really meant he was still between a rock and a hard place.

A loud explosion occurred next across the road that surprised both Greg and the assassin. He could not believe it but was definitely pleased that on a crest above the large boulder two workmen, nicknamed powder monkeys on the job site, were throwing sticks of dynamite near the assassin's location. This gave Greg enough time to relocate across the road, nearer the huge rock but still out of sight. The thug sprayed the hills behind him and then sprayed the rock where he thought Greg was at. This action gave away his position, now Greg reached for both his pistols, cocked them and rushed quickly to the site.

He heard a rattle sound and a scream, in an instant was around the rock with both guns drawn. The dynamite had dislodged a couple of big rattlers and threw them several feet near the assassins position behind the rock. As his attention was elsewhere firing his machine gun, his movements attracted the ire of the snakes. It was too late as he heard the rattle, one snake bit his thigh and the other lunged and bit his arm. When Greg saw what had happened, he quickly kicked the machine gun out of reach. The snakes were long gone but the tremors were starting to develop in the assassin's body. Greg had seen this many times before and as the poison crept inside his bloodstream, he would have many more convulsions. Before he put two bullets in him to quickly ease the pain, Greg almost felt sorry for him. No way to die out here without a real fight between them but his job now was a lot easier.

Vinny did not know what exactly was going on with his men. He heard many shots fired and saw workers actually throw dynamite sticks. He thought about getting back into his vehicle, shooting his way out and high tailing it back to Las Vegas. The sight of marshal Greg heading back to his vehicle and starting to come down the road looking for him changed his thinking fast. Getting into his car and speeding towards the dam site was the only alternative left. He would think of some way to get out of this predicament.

On the way back to his car, Greg picked up the machine gun and his shotgun. Proceeding slowly down the road and unsure of Vinny's whereabouts he scanned the rocks and bushes. A man was walking down from the rocks, as he got closer Greg knew he was one of the workers, his rail thin appearance befit many a dam worker these days. Maybe he was one of those powder monkeys that threw the dynamite sticks helping him out of one jam. "So glad to see you" the worker said excitedly "would you need any more of our help" pointing to other workers on the hillside. "Thank you for your assistance" Greg responded "but I can take care of this end now. How about alerting the other workers at the dam site about one more bad guy roaming around armed and dangerous." "We'll telephone the supervisors at the dam plus we are going down there to see if we can help" the worker responded while giving a thumbs up to Greg.

Greg continued down the road to a switch back that gave him a sweeping view of the road below. Greg observed a black jalopy speeding towards the dam, more than likely Vinny because it did not look like a work vehicle. He sped up but not so fast as to see if Vinny caused any more damage along the road to the dam site.

Communication was very fast as to what was happening away from the dam. Various workers heard gunfire in the canyon, thought something bad was going down and alerted their foremen and supervisors. When the call was received that marshal Greg was in trouble with gangsters near the dynamite storage area, the men knew what to do. To a man they gathered whatever work tools they had (pick axes, shovels, crescent wrenches, crow bars, etc.) and were ready to quit working and help Greg. Their foremen, keeping cooler heads and under a blistering work schedule, told them to keep working but stay vigilant. If they were in danger, high tail it off the work site until the situation was safe. Calls were made for more marshals in Boulder City but they would take some time to get at the dam site as they were busy with mysterious events in that city.

Vinny drove down the road to the worksite, not too fast to arouse suspicion but wanting to put some distance between himself and marshal Greg. The worksite was busy and clogged with trucks, men and materials. Perfect to blend in and disguise his whereabouts if he could just stay calm and focused. He scanned the canyon for a way out, his eyes searching the area for any possible exit routes. He could see a foot bridge with stairs on the canyon leading to some railroad tracks, this looked like the best option of limited options to get to the road above. Getting there would be a little difficult because once out of the vehicle his appearance would draw unwanted glances but with some luck and a .45 caliber pistol he liked his chances. He stopped his car and proceeded on foot to the area near the foot bridge.

Greg knew the area well but with the fast pace of the job to build the dam, the worksite was changing it seemed weekly. He continued in his car down the road, every once in a while checking with workers to see if they saw or heard anything unusual. With all the construction, trucks, jack hammers and men bustling around he thought it would be difficult to spot Vinny in all this organized chaos. Chance provided the opportunity when he heard shots fired ahead near an area with a foot bridge across the river. He was sure it was Vinny and that foot bridge could be a possible escape route. He quickly hurried to the site telling the workers who he was and to get down.

Vinny was climbing the zig zag stairs that led to the foot bridge across the river. He hiked up his coat collar and lowered the brim of his hat, trying not to bring attention to himself. His actions were suspicious to at least a couple of workers. They met him at the entrance to the footbridge and began to question him. Having not the time nor the inclination to answer them, he pulled his gun out and told them to beat it. The older worker backed up a bit with hands raised but the younger worker kept his eyes on Vinny and discreetly grasped his wrench in his back pocket.

Greg saw this unfolding on the side of the canyon, he was still too far away for a shot and he might hit the workers. In a command voice he shouted "Halt" to Vinny in particular but all the workers around him stopped what they were doing. Seeing that he had also drawn his pistol out of his holster, they also cringed down and some started to back away hurriedly. The shout was what distracted Vinny and he took his eyes off the workers to see if he could pinpoint Greg. This split second was all the younger worker needed; he swung the wrench at Vinny's wrist. Vinny by reflex shot the worker but the wrench came down hard on his wrist and he dropped the gun. Since they were near the edge of the canyon, the gun fell down to a small ledge at least 10 feet away.

Vinny wanted to retrieve the gun but now saw Greg running up the stairs quickly. He knew he had no time, so he decided to cross the footbridge and put some distance between him and Greg. His wrist was a painful black and blue mass, he tried to dismiss it as he sprinted as fast as he could across the bridge. Being a professional hit man he had a small .38 strapped to his ankle just for emergencies plus he could shoot with both hands. The US Army had really instructed him well.

Greg reached the area where the workers were near the footbridge. The older worker was trying to give first aid to the younger one. Greg kneeled down and saw the wound, chest high and near the heart, knew it would be eventually fatal but told the older man to keep pressure on it and help would get there soon. As Greg got up from kneeling down he saw Vinny almost on the other side of the footbridge. He quickened his pace across the bridge, wanting even more to apprehend or kill Vinny for likely killing a dam worker.

Vinny was across to the other side and he could see it was only a few feet up a incline to the railroad tracks. He quickly ran up the incline to the tracks and saw that a train was stopped about 50 yards from him. As Vinny sprinted towards the train his plan was to commandeer it and force the engineer to drive off the project. Little did he know that the tracks ended 100 yards from the train's location. The emergence of a vastly superior crane/cableway system across the canyon was leading to the dismantling of a prior train track system to deliver the concrete for the dam. Greg though was aware of this change and of the train tracks leading nowhere and a little smile creased along his weather beaten face. In one morning he would be able to make quite a dent in Mick's small criminal empire beginning to grow in Las Vegas; a day well spent he would say.

Vinny was at the engine when he stopped to catch his breath and look behind him to see if he could spot where Greg was. This was very advantageous for Greg as he had reached the top of the incline, got into a good crouching position and steadied his hand around the pistol. The second Vinny turned around Greg fired dead center at his assailant. The shot hit Vinny near the mid thigh, he hobbled around to the space between the engine and the first boxcar. It was bleeding pretty good so he used part of his torn shirt sleeve to fashion a pressure bandage quickly around the wound.

Pleased that his shot had found its mark but seeing Vinny duck around a railroad car, Greg moved slowly. Against the canyon wall there were a few stacked wooden crates. Greg took advantage of this cover and with gun in hand crept up to the train. With the stifling heat of the midday sun drenching everyone in sweat, the two combatants tried to conserve their energy for the final fight ahead. The surrounding workplace was also eerily silent as the workers bent and crouched behind any cover they could find until the ordeal was over.

Up above the site of conflict on the canyon wall was Jim "Two Bulls" Foxsom. As a high scaler his job was to prepare the canyon wall for the dam, which meant drilling holes for dynamite and then stripping them of loose rock. When he learned marshal Greg and some bad guys were shooting it out at the dam site, he stayed on his bosun chair just to see if he could help his friend below. During WW1 Greg was his first sergeant and he felt he owed his life to him for a few battles they were in. Jim had a good view of both of them below. He decided to pivot his rope and chair almost directly above the wounded bad guy's position. A scan of the rock canyon near him led him to believe that prying some loose rock with his crowbar might distract the shooter. Or if it fell on him, better yet for the marshal to quickly take advantage and subdue him.

Vinny took a deep breath, his painful leg thumping with each heart beat. He leaned out a little to his right peering for any sign of the marshal advancing. Not seeing anything he quickly ducked back and was preparing to look to his left against the canyon wall. At that moment he heard loud thuds above him, the top of the train car was absorbing some rocks. Maybe a small avalanche, he thought. He waited until the noise subsided then turned slowly to his left, gun in hand ready for anything. A shot nicked the train a few inches from where he was, apparently the marshal had caught up to him and was a good shot. "Come out with your hands up, you'll have a better chance of living" Greg yelled. "Like my two friends? No, I'll take my chances here and live to see another day" replied Vinny, shaking a little from the near hit. "I doubt that but at least I gave you a choice" Greg retorted as he crept along the canyon wall nearer to the train.

Vinny saw some metal rungs that led to the top of the train. His plan was to get above and possibly have a better shot at the marshal. As quietly as he could he climbed and then slid across the top. Some small rocks were on top also so he grabbed one and flung it against the canyon, hoping that the marshal would get distracted long enough for a good shot from him. He heard some movement about 45 degrees to his left. Still prone on top of the train, he turned quickly and unloaded his 5 shots in the direction of the noise. The noise was Nip who was curious as to what was going on. Scared but unhurt Nip fled to the safety of the diversion tunnels into the arms of a worker. One of the random shots Vinny fired only nicked Greg in the arm. Laying low until he heard all 5 shots fired, Greg figured now was the best time to bull rush the train. In a few strides with gun in hand he was against the boxcar hoping to keep Vinny off balance and unaware of his whereabouts.

Both men were on opposite sides of the train when a slew of rocks crashed down. Vinny hugged the side while Greg low crawled underneath the train. Vinny knew his only chance now was to quickly find the driver and force him to drive out of the canyon. When he began to run, Greg aimed and squeezed off two rapid fire shots at his lower legs. The fist one missed its mark but the second struck flesh a little lower than the knee. Vinny grimaced and turned his pistol sideways and quickly delivered three shots underneath the train.

After firing his shots Greg had rolled away in the space between two cars, stood up and readied himself for the final volley. He lunged around the corner, crouched and squeezed two rounds into the limping Vinny. The force of the bullets slammed him back a few feet like a staggered drunk. Vinny still raised his pistol for one last shot at the marshal. Before he could pull the trigger a large stone hit his chest and propelled him several feet off the canyon train roadbed. He had landed in one of the wooden dam forms and began to slowly sink in the recently poured cement mixture. A couple of the workers (puddlers they were called) who did not leave when the shooting started gathered their shovels and helped Vinny suffocate and left him buried in the concrete.

Greg watched all this happen and after giving a thumbs up to the workers in the form returned to the train. A yell came from above on the canyon wall near the train. Greg recognized Jim "Two Bulls" Foxsom on the bosun chair, so this was why the rocks were falling off the canyon wall. Greg waved back and uttered "Semper Fi" hoping that Jim would hear and as a fellow marine would return the pledge. Jim did and waved goodbye, scaling the rocks and jumping to a new position.

The workers who helped bury Vinny had quite a story to tell their co- workers but it was their foreman who told them to get the body out. It was already a rumor that some men were buried in the concrete. A body would decompose and air pockets would form, weakening the structure in certain area's and spell certain ruin for a dam in time. As they retrieved the body an informant for Mick who worked on the site saw the whole escapade with the marshal. He would eventually inform Mick what happened but continued to work so as not to arouse suspicion from his co-workers.

Greg was on his way back to his vehicle when applause started to erupt and men smiled and patted him on the back for a job well done. He acknowledged them and thanked them for their cooperation, not smiling too much for he knew the fight was not over. This round though seemed very gratifying he would admit later to his fellow marshals.

CHAPTER 12

Trouble Comes a Calling

Mick assembled four of his best bodyguards to a small room in a casino downtown. Mick had heard of Vinny's demise at the dam. He was not in a good mood, was angry and proceeded to lay out the problem in front of his men. "Three men have been giving me a problem lately" Mick stated slowly "and I want them taken care of." "Two are from Boulder City, one is at the dam worksite, I want them all dead." Narrrowing his eyes "Greg Conner, federal marshal, Nate Turner, a cook in Boulder City and Jim Foxsom, an Indian high scaler at the dam." "I don't care how you do it but they have cost me money and embarrassment for too long."

Mick leaves as the bodyguards deliberate how they will accomplish the plan. They know that in the hills around Boulder City there are many illegal stills and bootleggers. They decide to influence their contacts and set a trap for the federal marshal. It was agreed by all that Greg Conner would not delegate catching crooks to someone else, by all recent accounts he liked to round up criminals himself. Entering the city would pose little problems, one of the marshals was on the take. It was agreed to handle the cook first then the marshal and finally the Indian at the dam. Calls are made and the four headed outside to their two vehicles.

At the mess hall Nate was winding down his workday by preparing to cook the last few orders of a busy day. His day off would be spent in Las Vegas. He met a woman in a casino and after spending a lustful night at a cheap motel he could think of nothing else. The lady in question turned out to be the wife of Vinny, a good friend of Mick's. Once she confessed about the affair Mick took little time to add Nate to his killing list. A black man with a white woman was still not tolerated.

As the four bodyguards entered the mess hall Nate was in the back cooking up an order. Through a slot where the orders were picked up Nate saw the men enter. They looked rough and since he never saw them before was suspicious of their presence. He kept a low profile and thought about recently about his exploits in Las Vegas. Could there be a connection? The men were talking with a waiter of what he could not hear but he decided to get out the back. Better be safe than sorry in this situation. As he hurried out the back door, he heard shouts of "there he is" but in the alleys and corners he knew he could lose them.

Nate was running full speed down a dirt alley when one of the men spotted him. "He's over here" he heard one of them say so he quickly changed direction. Heart racing at the thought of being caught, his strides became longer and his cuts around houses more precise. Nate ducked around a newly built house then saw one of the men pull a gun out of his jacket. This was not looking good. Nate crept low and in the other direction when out of the corner of his eye he saw one of the federal marshals coming down the dirt road. The waiter had called them from the mess hall because of an uneasy feeling gleaned from their questions.

The bodyguards were converging where they thought Nate was when one of them saw the marshal. Not wanting to draw suspicion to them and knowing that they had further business to do, they calmly walked away. Seeing this, Nate waited till he was sure they were gone before he ventured out of hiding. "Sure glad to see you, do you know who those men were?" Nate breathlessly said. "Some of Mick's thugs, can't figure how they get in here so easy but they seem to be leaving. Were they after you?." "Seemed to be but I'm okay, just scared me white" Nate blabbered without realizing what he just said. "Be careful, these guys are deadly" he snickered at the response. Nate shook his hand and bid him goodbye. He thought about all his previous outings in Las Vegas, none ever got this serious. Visiting his newfound female friend on his day off was out of the question now.

They knew where he worked, probably would come back to finish the job. He told the manager at the mess hall some story about needing to visit family out East and laid low with some friends outside the town. He took advice and applied for a job at the dam, better safe than sorry.

The four henchmen circled around a few blocks to make sure the marshal was not following them. They all agreed that Mick would not like the news of Nate's survival. The need not to arouse too much suspicion led them to abandon the killing of Nate. Arriving at their vehicles, they agreed to be more precise in laying the trap for marshal Greg Conner.

The hills around the city were of volcanic origin and they were pockmarked with openings. Since there was no alcohol allowed in the city, an illegal operation began to fill the void. Hard to spot from the road, most required a trek up to the exact location. This put any law enforcement officer in a pickle and in the open. Earlier a telephone call had been made to a man who operated one of the stills. The plan was to leak this information about where the still was located to marshal Conner. His ego, from their report about him, led them to believe he and no one else would respond. All four would get into position near the still for a crossfire that should take him out of this world.

Marshal Conner was in his office when the call arrived. The one thing about bootleggers Greg counted on was their anti-competitive spirit: less of them means more profits. Snitching on others to accomplish this was commonplace. He took down the information, knew the area well since he covered it without ever finding the still. He got his hat, took a shotgun and a revolver and left the office towards his vehicle. A secretary asked if he needed any backup, he said no and keep the coffee warm.

The still was located high up a craggy prominence on the way to the worksite. The police knew bootlegging was going on, finding the stills were another matter. The area looked like the surface of the moon, little vegetation, more rocks and boulders. The four men took positions all around the still to allow no escape. They would wait with guns drawn for the precise time when the marshal was most vulnerable. The hot desert sun would also shield at least two of the men, which would be a plus in this situation. They waited silently to spring the trap on a seemingly unaware Greg Conner.

Greg stopped his vehicle off the side of the road and could see the outcropping of rocks. He got out, made sure the revolver was fully loaded and grabbed the shotgun on the passenger side. It was going to be a quite long haul up, he grabbed his old canteen from the war and headed up the hill. He turned off his radio so as to not to alarm anyone in the area. In these canyons any faint noise traveled a long way.

Halfway up Greg rested, drank a couple swigs of water from his canteen and plotted his way up to the location of the still. Around one rock he heard an ominous rattle, he froze in place, saw the rattler curled up. Greg knew he could blow it away with the shotgun but his surprise would be negated, so he stood still until the snake moved away. He continued to traverse a small footpath that became apparent after a few more rock scrambles.

The plan devised by the henchmen would have the bootlegger just outside the small eroded cave that held the still. Acting indifferent to the threat approaching, he would lure the marshal in hopefully unsuspecting. Their positions would allow a deadly crossfire that would surely kill Marshal Conner.

Although trying to be quiet, Greg knew that if someone was in the area the small rocks dislodged from his rambling could be heard. His strides became shorter and more precise, he was judging the best place to move forward and be quiet at the same time. Slow and agonizing although it was, Greg did not want to warn anyone else of his where-abouts. This blazing hot day he did not want to waste his sweat in a failed attempt to nab a criminal.

Slowly he crept around a rock, saw a man in front of a small cave-like opening, smelled the odor of grain alcohol and knew he had his man. "Hold it right there, feller" Greg forcefully said, "hands up, don't move or I'll drop you!." With his shotgun aimed midbody, slowly Greg walked a few paces in front of the man. Greg always liked to look directly in the eyes of those he arrested for if anything was amiss, the eyes would show movement.

Hands up, the man was trying to follow his instructions given and look directly at Greg but just a faint glance to the left alerted Greg to danger. A quick about-face with his trigger finger twitching, the shot hit him in the shoulder. He turned and fired the shotgun at a figure halfway obscured by a large rock. A shriek rang out in the direction he fired but not knowing how many men were out there, Greg ran for the nearest cover.

A large bush was nearby but before he made it behind another searing pain shot out from his lower leg. He was sure of two shooters, one of which he plugged, but how many more? Greg was reloading the shotgun when he heard voices from different directions asking "Did you see him?", "I think I got him", "I'm OK." They made enough noise to give Greg a good idea of their location. He grabbed a loose rock and flung it opposite of the location of the voices. Hoping that one of them might for an instant stay exposed, Greg aimed the shotgun this time. He squinted towards a large boulder, saw a blur appear and fired. A howl went up with some cursing, it was unprofessional mutterings mostly so Greg surmised he hit the bootlegger. Well, he accomplished his main mission, now he needed to get out of this jam.

The three remaining men signaled each other to concentrate fire on the large bush to finish the marshal. On three they would unload their pistols and machine guns from three directions for a crossfire effect. Painfully aware of this silence, Greg drew his revolver and with shotgun in the other hand, one shoulder and ankle in pain, reared up and ran towards the open. As he opened fire, remembrance of a remark made long ago during his time as a marine filled his senses. "C'mon men, do you want to live forever." He never had a chance but he managed to wing two of the thugs before a hail of bullets killed him.

All four men walked down a side trail that descended to a flat, sandy area where their vehicles were. One had a pronounced knee injury, two had minor upper arm wounds. Taking out the marshal was not as easy as they thought but Mick would be pleased. They agreed that the man with the injured knee should go back to Las Vegas. The other three would continue on with their final task; to wipe out the Indian called "Two Bulls." This particular person aided in the killing of one of Mick's bodyguards earlier. The plan was to follow the Indian from the worksite, abduct him, take him out to the desert, where they would beat him up and leave him to die.

The transportation of workers to and from the worksite required old double level 5 ton trucks holding up to 150 men. Taking a position on a hill overlooking this pickup point near the site, they waited and watched for their man. Seeing him enter the truck they started to follow in the car after the truck pulled out on the road. Long and winding for many miles the road finally straightened out and climbed to the town.

As the truck stopped to unload the men, the car with the henchmen stopped in good position to watch for Jim. They knew he was single and would be staying at the single men's dorm. Once he was spotted departing the truck and after a few conversations with fellow workers, he headed off for the dorm. They followed in the car and parked near the dorm. Agreeing that barging into the dorm was counter-productive, a couple of out-houses in the rear looked more promising. Of course patience would be required but being professionals waiting was part of the job. One man would loiter around the area and signal the other two when he saw the Indian walking towards the out-house.

About an hour later Jim came walking out of the dorm in the direction to the out-house. As he opened the wooden door with the half-moon cut in it out of the corner of his eye he saw an unfamiliar man. Paying more attention to his bladder than to his surroundings (unusual for an Indian) he shut the door behind him. At that exact moment the hand signal alerted the men in the car, one of them got out and hastily ran towards the out-house. Pulling out a revolver they were ready for Jim and as he exited was duly thumped by both on the head. Once Jim was on the ground they signaled the man in the vehicle. The vehicle stopped a few feet from them, they loaded Jim into the back seat and sped off.

It just so happened that four of Jim's Indian buddies were also in the dorm having played cards with Jim earlier. When Jim left to use the latrine the game continued but one friend, sensing something might be wrong went to the window. Seeing the fracas outside and the car speeding away he yelled to his buddies to join him at his car. Since there was only one road out of the city they knew where the car with Jim was headed. As they sped up to catch the car with Jim both cars came under surveillance of another federal marshal. He was at a body shop with his police car being worked on; he swiftly told the attendant to lower his car, got in, backed up and sped off.

The three bodyguards were speeding out of the city when the man in the back noticed that another auto could be seen far off getting closer. The passenger gunman saw a small dry wash to the left and notified the driver. This dry wash also had some cover and undulating paths connected to it. It was hoped that by turning down this dry wash they could lose whoever was following them. Proceeding down this dry wash was difficult, the tires were not gripping and progress was slow. After about 50 yards, they turned off and hid behind a rocky knoll. This hid them from the road. Watching a speeding car go by, they dragged Jim out of the back seat. The beating began almost immediately. Jim got in a few blows but that made the men even angrier.

Stopping their car, the Indians looked around for any sign of the car with Jim. "Let's retrace our path" one said so into reverse they went. The one with the best eyesight saw the dry wash, saw the tire tracks and told his friends to follow him. They got out of their car; hopefully a silent surprise would catch the perpetrators unawares. As they got closer they could hear the sounds of a scuffle. It was around the corner, over a good size knoll so they crept up close, peering over the top. The sight of Jim all bloody being tossed from one man to another and taking more shots drove them furious. Using hand signals two went around the opposite corners and waited until they heard the blood curdling howl of the two above.

Before they knew what was happening the henchmen knew they were in trouble. From above the two Indians leap was true, bringing down two of the goons quickly. The remaining man holding Jim threw him towards the Indian coming from the side. Running towards the vehicle where they left their guns (mistake #1) he almost made it before he was blindsided by the other Indian. Mistake #2 and a costly one, all the Indians were former marines from WW1, the Tuefulhunden to the Germans or devil dogs. The final and deadliest mistake, the bodyguards forgot to bring knives, the former leathernecks did not. Their intent was not to kill but to maim and they knew where to plunge the knife for the greatest effect. Quickly they dispatched their adversaries to the ground with major injuries. They helped Jim to his feet and started walking back to their vehicle, ignoring the cries from the fallen men.

Arriving at their vehicle they helped Jim into the backseat, got in themselves and drove towards the city. The marshal was driving the other direction, his siren came on, he turned around and sped towards the Indians. Approaching the vehicle he saw the condition of Jim in the backseat and unsnapped his revolvers safety strap. "I don't know where you guys have been but why were you speeding earlier?" The Indian driving the car said "We were just helping our friend" motioning to Jim in the back. "When he was kidnapped by some goons we quickly followed them out of the city where they left him to die in the desert." Jim was regaining consciousness, the marshal looked in the back; "Is that what happened, boy?" Jim nodded and said "It's all a blur but yes, they whipped me pretty good." Wincing at the pain he sat back and mumbled thanks to his friends in the car.

The marshal understood the life saving action of the Indian's friends, heck, he would have done the same for his. "You sure they left back to Las Vegas" he looked around the hills, "because these guys usually get their man or die trying?." Thinking fast one of the Indians responded saying "We did catch up to them, must have put the fear of God in them because they sped back to Vegas in a cloud of dust" as the others nodded in agreement. "Guess I'd do the same thing with four mad Indians on my trail" he snickered, "Go back to Boulder City, get some rest then back to work on that dam." He got back in his car and followed them to the city's entrance gate. The Indians all smiled, secure in the knowledge that just for a short time Semper Fi and never leave a man behind rang true once more.

CHAPTER 13

A Glimmer of Hope

I
t was a beautiful morning at the dam, the bright yellow sun casting whitish rays upon the worksite in Black Canyon. From a vantage point above the canyon Dave could see the multitude of workers below. Looking like tireless ants scurrying from one task to another all these workers were an important cog in building this gargantuan project. Dave was really proud of these men who endured numerous travails during the start of the Great Depression. They came to work under horrific and daunting work conditions. In lifting themselves up they also were lifting the country up out of a big hole. Dave was also remembering his fallen friend Greg from WW1 to a few weeks ago when he was killed by Mick's thugs. He felt safer whenever Greg was around, with so much still to do at the dam site Dave wished he was still here.

As Dave was reminiscing a long black sedan was approaching. As it stopped nearby Dave could see a burly man get out of the front, go to the back and opened the passenger door. Mick got out, was headed towards Dave when he remembered that Susan was also in the back, turned back toward the vehicle and offered his hand to help Susan exit the vehicle. As they both approach Dave notices that Mick looked a little happy, even though Dave knows that a few of Mick's goons took a bruising with a fight with Jim's friends. "Just thought I'd come out and see you before I leave to Chicago" Mick said as he eyed the men below working. "You might want to know that a Mr. Al Capone wants me to join his crew up there, heard about my success in Las Vegas and wants some of that in Chicago." "That's nice" Dave said as he eyed Susan as she got near the edge of the overlook which dropped down 30 feet to another loop in the road. Noticing the closeness of Susan to the edge, Mick responded "Would not mind going there alone." Susan pulled back a few feet. "You wouldn't dare!" "Try me, you know you are beginning to bore me" Mick quipped as he looked down on the men and the worksite.

They all looked down on the worksite mesmerized by the hard work of the men. Mick was a little jealous of Dave in his position of foreman, men would follow his orders without coercion. If only he commanded the same respect with his men maybe he would have accomplished more in Las Vegas. Even though he knew he could not live in Mick's shoes, Dave was a little jealous of the material rich trappings it supplied. The accomplishments of each could not bridge the divide that separated them since that fateful day in childhood with the flood. "Well, it's about time Susan and I get started going east to our new home" Mick said as he started back to the automobile. He knew the words "new home" would eat at his brothers heart but he did not care.

Susan did not automatically go with Mick to the car, instead Susan handed a note to Dave. It said "I know my behavior has not been very kind to you, I'm sorry but I like pretty, expensive things. Mick can give me what I want but not necessarily what I need." As she handed Dave the note, she hugged him and swiftly turned to the car, knowing that Mick would probably be very mad at what he saw.

Dave followed her with his gaze to the car, saw her get in and the car sped away. Dave felt sorry for her, he sensed a change in her speech and behavior since they met again. The divide he felt with Mick he did not feel with Susan, maybe since he never gave up on her the divide could be repaired. "Sorry for my past life, hurt a lot of people, including you but hang in there and we will see each other again. I am weary of this life with Mick and long for a simpler life with you in the future."

Dave looked up, tears in his eyes trying to see if he could see any trace of the car. He remembered the young Susan and how she made him feel, this was almost the same. As he was remembering the past Dave also recalled a time in the past when a pond and fishing were the best things life offered. A smile came upon his face when recalling the two beavers who created the pond with their earthen branch dam.

Looking down at the worksite he could envision the similarities between the two endeavors; animals changing nature for their benefit and man changing nature for theirs. A worker seeing Dave on the hill shouted "Where do you want this load of pipes?" "Over there" Dave pointed, "where the cable crane can get it to the bottom." Dave knew he was part of something big but in a part of his mind, he longed for something more.

The Hoover Dam, one of the 20th century's greatest engineering wonders was 85 years old this year.

HOOVER DAM CONTRIBUTIONS

The following is a list of states that contributed material from tin cups to steel gates to help build Hoover Dam during the 1930's. The labor force came from all over the United States during the Great Depression of the 30's. The average worker was 32 years of age, 40% were unmarried, and the average daily workforce was over 3500 men. During the peak building years of 1933-35 there were over 5218 men. 21,374 total workers (source: usbr.gov)

Basin States: Arizona, Nevada, Colorado, California, New Mexico (river does not pass through), Wyoming, Utah and finally Mexico.
Source of water: Rocky Mountain National Park at Grand Lake.

Native Americans

Native American High Scalers were responsible for drilling, blasting, and the smoothing out a portion of Black Canyon so that the foundations of the Dam and power plant could be laid.
Southwestern tribes such as the Yaqui, Crow, Navajo, and Apache provided the inspiration for symbols for the terrazzo floor in the Dam and power plant. These 125 designs were incorporated into the larger Art Deco design that decorates the Dam. The designs symbolized power and the generation of electricity by water.

ALABAMA

243 workers.
Lumber.
Bulkhead gate hoists and butterfly valves for power plant, emergency gates & needle valves butterfly valves and butterfly valve bulkheads for power plant. for canyon wall outlet works. Hardie-Tynes Mfg. Co., Birmingham.
Trash racks for the intake towers, Ingalls Iron Work Co., Birmingham.
Upper & lower entrance liners for intake towers. Goslin-Birmingham Mfg. Co., Inc, Birmingham.
Battery charging sets, battery control switchboard. Goslin-Birmingham Mfg. Co., Inc, Birmingham.

ARIZONA

643 workers.
Real estate for ½ of Hoover Dam.
Rock and gravel to mix with Portland Cement to make concrete.
State commission officials and Governor.
Water from many tributaries which feed the Colorado River.

ARKANSAS

191 workers.
Chicken for Anderson Mess Hall in Boulder City.
Lumber.

CALIFORNIA

5055 workers.
Boulder Canyon Dam power plant and appurtenant works. Six Companies, Inc main offices, *San Francisco*
Three of original six companies:
    Bechtel from Oakland
    Kaiser from San Francisco
    McDonald-Kahn from Los Angeles
Igneous Rock (black diorite) for terrazzo floors, Santa Ana.
Power for construction, Nevada-California Power Co., Southern Sierras Power Co., Newberry Electric Co., Los Angeles. (ran lines too/from San Bernardino, CA)

Turbines and governors, Pelton Water Wheel Co., (offices) San Francisco.
Railroad from Las Vegas to Boulder City, Union Pacific Railroad, Los Angeles & Salt Lake Co., Los Angeles.
Drum gates & drum gate control mechanisms for spillway, Cylinder gate hoists for intake towers, *Consolidated Steel Corp., Los Angeles.*
Fabricating pipe & fittings, Pipe, fitting, valves, & appurtenances,, *Associated Piping & Engineering Co. ltd., Los Angeles.*
Disconnecting switches (287.5 kilovolt) for power plant, *Bowie Switch Co., San Francisco.*
Bulkhead and stony gates, Consolidated *Steel Co. Ltd., San Francisco.*
Brass pipe pieces, *Grinnell Co., Inc. Los Angeles.*
High pressure gates & conduit linings for U.S. Plug in tunnel No. 1, 30" sphere valves for station service penstocks, 86" parafox emergency gates for tunnel plug outlet works. *Joshua Hendy Iron Works, San Francisco.*

Overhead revolving cranes for intake towers. *Judson pacific Co., San Francisco.*
Portland cement. *Riverside Cement Co., Los Angeles.*
Hydraulic control board and position transmitters for power plant, *Square D. Co., Inc. Los Angeles.*
Deep well turbine pumping units for Dam and power plant, *Victor Equipment Co., Los Angeles.*
Surfacing Black Canyon highway and adjacent parking areas. *E.L. Yeager,. Riverside or Boulder???*

COLORADO
467 workers.
Western headquarters for the Department of the Interior, Bureau of Reclamation,
(Government agency that supervised the Building of Hoover Dam), *Denver.*
Scientific testing of materials used in building the Dam and appurtenant works, *Denver.*
Sewage and water purification plant, *Stearns Roger Mfg. Co., Denver*
Marble for terrazzo floor, from headwaters of the Colorado River, Rocky Mountains.
Terrazzo work for boulder Dam power plant. *J.B. Martina Mosaic Co., Denver.* Spec # 642; 12/24/34. S (1936 book, material and labor chart) $51, 7170.work started 4/18/36.
Designer Alan Tupper True created terrazzo motif designs of Native American origin. *Denver.*
Power plant operation including transmission facilities & built power lines, *City of Los Angeles & Southern California*
Generator, 4 turbines, generator voltage, oil circuit breakers, *Allis-Chalmers Mfg Co. Denver.*
2 generate, power transformer. General Electric Co., Denver
Generators for units N-5 & N-6. and 287.5 kilovolt lighting arresters. *General Electric Co., Schenectady.*
Structural steel for power plant, *American Bridge Co., Denver.*
Bus structure, lighting arresters supports, disconnecting switch supporting structures, *American Bridge Co., Denver.*
Station service penstock for power plant; The *Babcock & Wilcox Co., Denver*
150 ton cableway car transfer cradle, *The Babcock & Wilcox Co., Denver*
250 volt direct current distribution switchboards. *Graybar Electric Co., Denver.*
Control cable supports for power plant, *The Midwest Steel & Iron Works Co., Denver*
Turbines & governors for power plant. *Pelton Water Wheel Co., San Francisco.*
Portland cement. *Union Portland Cement Co., Denver.*
Pipe & fittings for A-8, *Standard Sanitary Mfg. Co., Denver.*

CONNECTICUT
467 workers.
Sureties on performance bond for Six Companies Inc., Hartford Accident & Indemnity Co., Hartford
Crescent wrenches for all workers, Stanley Tool Co., Hartford.
Elevators in Powerhouse, Otis Elevator Co., Farmington.
Purchasing offices, *Denver.*

DELAWARE
1 worker.
Aerial photography of topography & ground surveys, Aerotopograph Corp. of America, *Washington DC.*

FLORIDA
66 workers.
Cypress wood for arches and tunnels inside the Dam.
Marble for terrazzo floor. Confirm? Company?

GEORGIA
115 workers.
"White Georgia" white marble for terrazzo floors
Lumber for Dam and power plant.

IDAHO
599 workers.
Morrison-Knudson Co., one of Six Companies, *Boise.*   ???????????????????? What do????????
Lumber for Dam and power plant.

ILLINOIS
487 workers.
Governors for 115,000 h.p. turbines, governors for units N-5 & N-6, Woodward Governor Co., *Rockford.*
Automatic telephone apparatus, American Automatic Electric Sales Co., *Chicago.*
Tractors, Caterpillar Tractor Co., *Peoria.*
Structural steel for the Dam, Bethlehem Steel Co., *Gary.*
Dump trucks, International Harvester.

Insulated cable and telephone wire, General Cable Co., Chicago.
2300 volt switching equipment, Delta Star Electric Co., Chicago.
Concrete mixing equipment, 3rd plant, C.S. Hohmson Co., Champaign

INDIANA
159 workers.
Penstock pipe 30' in diameter, 2 ¾" thick boiler plate steel.
Engineered by Purdue University, *Lafayette*.
Structural glass work, Sanitary Construction Co., *Indianapolis*.
Elevator shaft in Visitors Center, Frontier Kemper Construction Inc., *Evansville*
Structural steel for the Dam, Bethlehem Steel Co., *Gary*.
Steel plates & shapes for penstock, Illinois Steel Co. *Gary*. (pg 136, 1936)

IOWA
181 workers.
Gasoline locomotive, Davenport Desler Corp., *Davenport*.
Metal work & concrete mixing plant, Pittsburgh Des Moines Steel Co., *Des Moines*.
President Herbert Hoover's birthplace and home of presidential library.
    (31st president of the United States. Humanitarian, engineer, conservationist, and statesman).

KANSAS
327 workers.
Petroleum products, work boots for workers.

KENTUCKY
103 workers.

LOUSIANA
85 workers.
Hemp rope for high scalers.

MAINE
18 workers.
Construction superintendent & master Dam builder, Frank T. Crowe, *University of Maine*.
Lumber for the Dam & Power plant.

MARYLAND
66 workers.
Sureties for bond for Six Companies, Fidelity & Deposit Co., *Baltimore*.
Miscellaneous 2300 & 16,500 volt switching equipment for electricity, Wolfe & Mann Mfg. Co., *Baltimore*.

MASSACHUSETTS
114 workers.
Motor operated gate valves, Chapman Valve Mfg. Co., *Indian Orchard*
Insulated cable. Simplex Wire & Cable Co., *Boston*.

MICHIGAN
251 workers.
Cranes and hoists, Shaw Box Crane & Hoist Co., *Muskegon*.
Ventilation and air cooling equipment, six exhaust fans for ventilating, American Blower Corp., *Detroit*.
Dump trucks, Ford & Chevy, General Motors Co., *Detroit*
Lumber for Dam and power plant.
Aluminum metal sash windows & equipment. The Kawneer, *Niles*.

MINNESOTA
208 workers-
In-house power plant generators, Electric Machinery Co., *Minneapolis*.
Lumber for Dam and Power Plant.
Horizontal alternating current generator, Electric Machinery Co., *Minneapolis*.

MISSISSIPPI
50 workers.
Lumber.

MISSOURI
548 workers.
Hatch frames and covers, structural steel, rails for turbine gallery crane runway. . *Stupp Bros Bridge Iron Co., St. Louis*
Portable transformer track for power plant, *Kansas City Structural Steel Co., Kansas City.*
Bulkhead gates for turbine draft tubes. *The Mississippi Valley Structural Steel Co., St. Louis.*
Station service power and lighting transfers. *Moloney Electric Co., St. Louis.*

MONTANA
340 workers.
Lumber for Dam and power plant.

NEBRASKA
157 workers.
Miscellaneous metal work for power plant, Omaha Steel Works, Omaha.

NEVADA
5522 workers. ¼ of total work force.
Real estate for ¼ Hoover Dam.
Earthwork, concrete and erection of warehouse, Storm & Mahoney Inc., *Las Vegas*
Employment offices for laborers, Las Vegas.
Union Pacific Railroad from Las Vegas to Boulder City.
(mTrack Bracken, NV thru Boulder City and rim of Black Canyon)
Construction of high school building in Boulder City, White & Alter Construction Co., Elko
State commissioner, Governor Richard Kirman Sr.
Telephone lines, Southern Nevada Telephone Co., Las Vegas
(Connected Black Canyon w/Boulder City, Las Vegas, and beyond.)
Food for workers on project, Anderson Mess Hall (company who provided food for Hollywood actors), Boulder City.
    Room & Board at $1.60 per adult male. Workers would over pack included lunch and distribute to other needy workers
    families.
Penstock Fabrication, *Bechtel.*
House wreckers, *Wattis-Decker Co. (pg 55, 1936 A.P.H.)*
Paving Black Canyon Highway *E.L. Yeager.*
Highway between Las Vegas & Boulder City, *State of NV.*

NEW HAMPSHIRE
14 workers.
Granite for Terrazzo Floors.

NEW JERSEY
104 workers.
150 ton cable way furnished and erected, Lidgerwood Mfg. Co., *Elizabeth.*
Carbon dioxide fire extinguishing equipment, C-O Two Fire Equipment Co., *Newark.*
Pelton Water Wheel in-house generators for power plant), *Atlantic City.*

NEW MEXICO
109 workers.
Boulder City grading, paving, surfacing, curbs, gutters, sidewalks, sewers and water systems.
    New Mexico Construction Co., *Albuquerque.*
Terra cotta tile for 705 gallery used for Dam tour.
Tributary for Colorado River, San Juan.

NEW YORK
221 workers.
55,000 h.p. turbine for power plant. Newport News Shipbuilding & Dry Dock Co., New York.
Steel plate outlet pipes, discharge guides for 72" needle valves for tunnel, plug out works, Babcock & Wilcox Co., office in
    New York City.
Bronze winged statues, General Bronze Corp., *Long Island City.*
Metal doors, railings and structural and architectural metal work, General Bronze Co., Long Island City

84" needle valve discharge guide, American Locomotive Co., *Schenectady*
Generators for power plant, General Electric Co., *Schenectady*.
Ventilating duct systems without fans, The Electric Ventilation & Engineering Co., Inc, New York.
Valves for power plant &Fabricated brass pipe and fittings and special fabricated, The Greene- Wolf Co., Inc. Brooklyn.

NORTH CAROLINA
120 workers.
Tables, chairs, and work clothing.
Lumber.

NORTH DAKOTA
workers unknown if any.
Food products, cereals and grains.

OHIO
260 workers.
Turbine gallery crane, *Alliance Machine Co., Alliance.*
Aluminum metal rolling doors, *The Kinnear Mfg. Co., Columbus.*
Automatic elevators for canyon wall valve houses, Electric elevators for canyon wall valve houses, *Haughton Elevator Co.,*
       Toledo.
Steel for 30" diameter diversion pipes, Babcock & Wilcox, *Baberton.*
Structural steel for Dam, *Bethel Steel Co., Youngstown.*
Transformers for power plant and Boulder City, *Standard Transformer Co., Warren.*

OKLAHOMA
581 workers.
Transmission towers for city of Los Angeles, Tulsa Boiler & Machinery Co., *Tulsa*
Petroleum products.

OREGON
273 Workers.
87 board feet of lumber, 37 MILLION
J.F Shay (Shea)
Pacific Richmond

PENNSYLVANIA
238 workers.
Aerial topography and ground surveys, *Brock & Weymouth, Philadelphia.*
Bulkhead gates for intake towers, *Bethlehem Steel Co., Bethlehem.*
Stony gates hoists, Reading Iron Co., *Reading*; structural steel, Bethlehem Steel Co., *Bethlehem.*
Transmission towers & switchyard structures (circuits 2, 4, 5), *American Bridge Co., Pittsburgh.*
Four turbines, *I.P. Morris, Philadelphia.*
Reinforcing tie rods, *Midvale C., Nicetown.*
Cold pin steel (hot rolled & normalized, Penstocks?) , *Carnegie Steel Co., Pittsburgh.*
Penstock Bulkheads & bulkhead flange bolts for penstocks (only part of need), Erie Forge Co., Erie.
23,000 volt bus structure. I-T-E Circuit breaker Co., Philadelphia.
Structural steel for intake tower bridges, McClintock Marshall Co., Bethlehem.
Structural steel supports & gratings for tunnel walkways. Reliance Steel Products Co., Rankin.
Water jet ejectors. *Schutte & Koerting Co., Philadelphia.*
30" sphere valves for station service penstock. S. Morgan Smith Co. *York.*
72" needle valves and drilling templates for tunnel plug outlet works. *Thomas Spacing Machine Co., Pittsburgh.*,
Upper and lower cylinder gates for intake towers, generators, generators for A- 6 & A-7, 287.5 kilovolt oil circuit breakers and
       generator neutral reactors and oil circuit breakers, main control room equipment and clock supply power equipment,
       power transformers for units N-5 & N-6, 23,000 volt bus structure & generator neutral grounding reactor and oil circuit
       breaker, *Westinghouse Electric & Mfg. Co., East. Pittsburgh.(-or- Denver, Colorado??? Offices)*

RHODE ISLAND
8 workers.
Granite for terrazzo floor.

SOUTH CAROLINA
29 workers.
Work clothing.
Lumber for Dam.

SOUTH DAKOTA
58 workers.
Food products, cereals and grains.
Lumber, *Black Hills*.

TENNESSEE
121 workers.
Butterfly valves and internal differential control valves for spillway, Johnson City Foundry & Machine Co., Johnson City.

TEXAS
604 workers.
Oil and petroleum products, citrus and vegetables for Anderson Mess Hall in
      Boulder City.

UTAH
1165 workers.
Black marble for terrazzo floor.
*One of the original Six companies, Utah Construction Co., *Ogden*.
(railroad construction, tunneling, and dam construction)
Tributary of Colorado River(Virgin).
Transmission lines, Pickering Bros., *Salt Lake City*.
Construction of school in Boulder City, I.M. Bay, *Junction City*.
Construction of six 3 & 4 room residences in Boulder City, Louis J Bowers, *Salt Lake City*.

VERMONT
6 workers.
Oak.
Cardiff green marble for terrazzo floor.

WASHINGTON
642 workers.
Highway, Boulder City to dam site, Genera Construction Co., *Seattle*.
Tow boat for Lake Mead Reservoir. Tregoning Boat Co., *Seattle*.
Lumber.
Control panels for generators (modern), Schweitzer Engineering Lab, *Pullman*.

WEST VIRGINIA
73 workers.
Lumber.

VIRGINIA
44 workers.
Turbine for power plant, Newport News Ship Building & Dry Dock Co., *Milwaukee*.
Lumber.

WISCONSIN
171 workers.
Four turbines for power plant, shafts for generators, Allis-Chalmers Mfg. Co., Milwaukee.
460 and 115 volt alternating current control equipment, Cutler-Hammer, Inc., *Milwaukee*.
Overhead traveling cranes for power plant, Harnischfeger Sales Corp., *Milwaukee*.
Miscellaneous metal work for power plant, Worden-Allen Co., Milwaukee.

WYOMING
161 workers.
Lumber.
Water from tributary to Colorado River(Green River).

Work Force

The following information was taken from a newspaper article in the '30's. It shows the breakout, by state, of where the people who built the dam came from.

State	Number of Men	State	Number of Men
Alabama	243	Nebraska	157
Arizona	643	Nevada	5522
Arkansas	191	New Jersey	104
California	5055	New Mexico	109
Connecticut	467	New York	221
Colorado	467	New Hampshire	14
Delaware	1	North Carolina	120
Florida	66	Ohio	260
Georgia	115	Oklahoma	581
Idaho	599	Oregon	273
Illinois	487	Pennsylvania	238
Indiana	159	Rhode Island	8
Iowa	181	South Carolina	29
Kansas	327	South Dakota	58
Kentucky	103	Tennessee	121
Louisiana	85	Texas	604
Maine	18	Utah	1165
Maryland	66	Virginia	44
Massachusetts	114	Vermont	6
Missouri	548	Washington	642
Michigan	251	West Virginia	73
Minnesota	208	Wisconsin	171
Mississippi	50	Wyoming	161
Montana	340	Foreign workers	116

Total = over 21,000.

Last Reviewed: 9/10/2004

FOREIGN WORKERS
116 workers.

Norway: Norwegian Born Oskar Hansen (immigrant/naturalized) who sculpted the 30' Winged Statues of the Re
memorial Bronze plaques, star map, and base relief on towers (honor 96 industrial accidents.

England: Gordon B. Kaufman. Architect & Artistic designer of Dam's beauty. Influenced by design elements o
Modernism / Art Deco aesthetics. Counter Balance the engineers focus on "functionality rather th
aesthetics" Simplified Dam's original design. Replaced plans for gaudy ornamentation with mode
flowing Lines and Art Deco design. *London.*

Czech: Retaining walls created from rubble on slopes of Black Canyon. FIND SOURCE?????

111 black workers segregated from living in Boulder City.
8 Native American workers, 6 of which were Apache.
No Asians by law.

SIX COMPANIES
Consortium of 6 Major Western companies.

Morrison-Knudson Co., Boise, Idaho
Road and Dam construction, expertise

J.F. Shea Co., Portland, Oregon
Tunnels and underground work

Pacific Bridge Co., Portland, Oregon
Underwater construction

McDonald & Kahn, Los Angeles, CA
Concrete buildings, industrial plants, sky scrapers

Bechtel-Kaiser-Warren Brothers, Oakland, CA. (Listed at W.A. Bectel & Harry J. Kaiser.
Road & trail road construction
Cooling plant

Utah Construction Co., Ogden, Utah
Railroad construction, tunneling, and dam construction

Bid $ 48,890,955

Warren Harding, 29th President
Calvin Coolidge 30th President 8/2/23 – 3/4/29
Herbert Hoover, Secretary of commerce under Warren Harding (1921-1923) and Calvin Coolidge. 3/5/21-8/21/28
Herbert Hoover, 31st President. 3/4/1929-3/4/1933
Franklin D. Roosevelt, 32nd President. 3/4/1933-4/12/1945

1928 Colorado River Compact
"equitable split of rivers water"
"federal gov't representative"
"instrumental in negotiations"
Signed 11/24/1922. Final ratification 6/25/1929

THE END

www.ingramcontent.com/pod-product-compliance
Lightning Source LLC
Chambersburg PA
CBHW020325130626
46549CB00003B/1021